The Survivor Personality

THE
Survivor
Personality

Why Some People Are Stronger, Smarter,
and More Skillful at Handling
Life's Difficulties . . .
and How You Can Be, Too

AL SIEBERT, PhD

Contributing Editors
Kristin Pintarich and Molly Siebert

A PERIGEE BOOK

A PERIGEE BOOK
Published by the Penguin Group
Penguin Group (USA) Inc.
375 Hudson Street, New York, New York 10014, USA
Penguin Group (Canada), 90 Eglinton Avenue East, Suite 700, Toronto, Ontario M4P 2Y3, Canada
(a division of Pearson Penguin Canada Inc.)
Penguin Books Ltd., 80 Strand, London WC2R 0RL, England
Penguin Group Ireland, 25 St. Stephen's Green, Dublin 2, Ireland (a division of Penguin Books Ltd.)
Penguin Group (Australia), 250 Camberwell Road, Camberwell, Victoria 3124, Australia
(a division of Pearson Australia Group Pty. Ltd.)
Penguin Books India Pvt. Ltd., 11 Community Centre, Panchsheel Park, New Delhi—110 017, India
Penguin Group (NZ), 67 Apollo Drive, Rosedale, North Shore 0632, New Zealand
(a division of Pearson New Zealand Ltd.)
Penguin Books (South Africa) (Pty.) Ltd., 24 Sturdee Avenue, Rosebank, Johannesburg 2196,
South Africa
Penguin Books Ltd., Registered Offices: 80 Strand, London WC2R 0RL, England

While the author has made every effort to provide accurate telephone numbers and Internet addresses at
the time of publication, neither the publisher nor the author assumes any responsibility for errors, or for
changes that occur after publication. Further, the publisher does not have any control over and does not
assume any responsibility for author or third-party websites or their content.

PRINTING HISTORY
Practical Psychology Press edition / 1993
First Perigee trade paperback edition / September 1996
Revised Perigee trade paperback edition / July 2010

Revised Perigee trade paperback ISBN: 978-0-399-53592-5

The Library of Congress has cataloged the first Perigee edition as follows:

The survivor personality / Al Siebert : foreword by Bernie Siegel.— 1st Perigee ed.
    p.   cm.
"A Perigee Book."
Previously published : Portland, Or. : Practical Psychology Press © 1993.
Includes bibliographical references and index.
ISBN 0-399-52230-1
1. Life change events—Psychological aspects.   2. Self-help techniques.   3. Conduct of life.   I. title.
[BF637.L53S54 1996]
158'.1—dc20   96-11324 CIP

PRINTED IN THE UNITED STATES OF AMERICA

10   9   8   7   6   5   4   3   2

Neither the publisher nor the author is engaged in rendering professional advice or services to the
individual reader. The ideas, procedures, and suggestions contained in this book are not intended as a
substitute for consulting with your physician. All matters regarding your health require medical
supervision. Neither the author nor the publisher shall be liable or responsible for any loss or damage
allegedly arising from any information or suggestion in this book.

Most Perigee books are available at special quantity discounts for bulk purchases for sales promotions,
premiums, fund-raising, or educational use. Special books, or book excerpts, can also be created to fit
specific needs. For details, write: Special Markets, Penguin Group (USA) Inc., 375 Hudson Street, New
York, New York 10014.

LAWRENCE ALBERT ("AL") SIEBERT

At the moment I was introduced to Al, I was captivated by his quiet, gentle, yet playful spirit that twinkled in his eye. I often watched and listened as he responded and interacted with people. I observed the deep connection they felt with him and his work, and I gained immense respect for his clear insight into how humans survive and thrive. Al and I both acknowledged that our connection was much more than our human brains could reason. Sharing six years of marriage with Al was more than any lifetime experience could provide.

This edition of *The Survivor Personality* is dedicated to the memory of Al Siebert, PhD, and his life's work of more than forty years as a pioneer in survivor and resiliency research. I admired witnessing how Al was hitting his stride as an internationally recognized and sought-after resiliency expert and consultant to organizations such as the World Trade Center Survivor's Network, the U.S. Army Medical Service Corps Provider Resiliency Training, the federal Eastern Management Development Center, Northwest tribal gatherings, and more. Unfortunately, Al was taken from all of us—you, his family, and me—before he felt his contribution was complete. He was comforted in the knowledge that people will continue to learn and grow from his survivor personality and resiliency research.

It is my desire that this book will enrich your life by showing you that you can learn the skills necessary to survive and thrive in any life experience.

—MOLLY SIEBERT

CONTENTS

This book is a survivor. For more than fifteen years and in eight different languages, it has inspired those around the world who reach for its universal message: that we all possess, instinctively, everything we need to survive, adapt, and thrive. Survivors have learned it is in the development of everyday skills that will better allow them to overcome adversity and challenge by providing a reservoir of responses from which to draw. Survivors know that experiencing crisis will often enable inborn strengths they didn't know they had. Survivors have learned to search for the gift in their difficult situation.

In today's world, we all need to be survivors. It is not just of extreme situations but also in daily life, work, and health. The wisdom captured within these pages is timeless and crosses situational boundaries. While the survivor personality is something everyone feels, we often don't know how to manifest it into the survival skills necessary for surviving and thriving in our own lives. When talking with people about the *survivor personality*, some will respond, "I have that" but are unable to articulate exactly what it means. Al Siebert removed the guesswork.

We humans have a wonderful advantage over other creatures. Our brains give us the ability to respond with conscious choice to events in our lives instead of being led by a simple, reflexive reaction that may do us in. The awareness of our conscious response to adversities and challenges can provide us with the choice to respond mindfully instead of automatically.

The type of attitude you develop toward change determines your level of survival. Understanding basic theories of why and how to change the way you react in stressful situations and practicing the exercises in this book will lead you to discover your inborn skills as well as how to become change proficient. You will see that the proficiencies necessary to cope, adapt, survive, and thrive through adversity are largely the same ones you use every day. You will find that an experience that once may have drained you emotionally can be made emotionally nutritious. A difficulty that might have broken you can be turned into one of the best things that ever happened to you.

Al had unique experience and perspective gathering his life's work on survival and resiliency. We believe this revised edition of *The Survivor Personality* will give you a better understanding of why developing your own survivor personality traits is essential and provide you with the tools you need to do so.

KRISTIN PINTARICH
MOLLY SIEBERT

FOREWORD

I was raised by parents who taught me about survival behavior. My father's father died when he was a child, and my father told me that it was one of the best things that ever happened to him because it taught him how to survive. My mother, in times of adversity, would tell me, "It was meant to be. God is redirecting you. Something good will come of this." It never failed to amaze me how often God did something to prove my mother right.

Most of us are not trained by parents, teachers, or religions to survive. If you are one of the fortunate few taught by family or circumstances the lessons of survival, then this book will confirm what you already know. If you have yet to discover within yourself those qualities that seem evident in survivors, then this book will show you not only what they are but how you can access and use them for yourself.

So many people complain that life is unfair, but that very fact proves just how fair it can be. Life doesn't discriminate. Everyone's life contains difficulties, and Al Siebert, with his wisdom and experience, shows you not only how to survive but how to thrive in the face of adversity.

A few people recover when their physicians expect them to die. I asked many of these survivors, "Why didn't you die when you were supposed to?" I learned that their recovery was not luck, a miracle, or because of an error in diagnosis. They all knew they participated in their survival. It is the same for those who make it through natural disasters and other catastrophic events; they know they were not just lucky.

There are qualities that survivors possess, and they can be described and learned. No one can make you a survivor and thriver. You have to have the desire and inspiration. No one can change you. Only you can do that, but the script—the road map—is here for you to follow. Many others have gone before you on this journey. They have trudged through the deep snow leaving a path for you. Stepping in their footsteps will make the journey easier. You don't have to be a pathfinder.

Why would you want to make the effort? Well, which is the better choice, self-love or self-neglect and self-destruction? The truth is, it is not selfish to care for yourself. If you don't, who will? Part of surviving is knowing you are not just the role you are playing. You need a life with the self-esteem and self-worth that go with it.

There are certain qualities I would like to emphasize before you journey into the wisdom in this book. Survivors are not afraid to have feelings. You must be in touch with your body and its messages. Numbing or distracting yourself may stop pain temporarily, but it won't help you survive. Learn from pain. Know that it can be a wake-up call, gift, or new beginning. If you do not use your pain, you will lose yourself and your identity.

Please never forget to see the world through the eyes of a child. A childlike sense of humor is a vital necessity if one is to survive life.

Learn from survivors about the importance of empathy and compassion.

Allow your creativity and intuition to guide you. Live "to

now." Survivors don't live in the past or the future. I guarantee that if you live in the moment, a voice will begin to speak to you with creative thoughts and ideas that will amaze you.

Get ready, dear reader, to embark on a personal journey to become a co-creator and participate in the survival of your self and your planet. When you have finished the book, find a survivor who can be a role model for you. For me it is Lassie: whenever I run into difficulties I ask myself, "What would Lassie do now?" But wherever you find your role model, your inspiration, or your motivation, you will discover that the essence of survival behavior is a reverence for all life and a compassionate response to all suffering.

PEACE . . .

BERNIE SIEGEL, MD,
author of *Love, Medicine, and Miracles*;
Faith, Hope and Healing; and
How to Live Between Office Visits, and many others

ONE

Life Is Not Fair

And That Can Be Very Good for You

WHEN you are hit by adversity or have your life disrupted, how do you respond? Some people feel victimized. They blame others for their plight. Some shut down. They feel helpless and overwhelmed. Some get angry. They lash out and try to hurt anyone they can.

A few, however, reach within themselves and find ways to cope with the difficult circumstance. They eventually make things turn out well. These are life's best survivors, those people with an amazing capacity for surviving crises and extreme difficulties. They are resilient and durable in distressing situations. They regain emotional balance quickly, adapt, and cope well. They thrive by gaining strength from adversity and often convert misfortune into a gift.

Are life's best survivors different from other people? No. They survive, cope, and thrive better because they are better at using the inborn capabilities possessed by all humans.

Surviving and Thriving:
Using Your Inborn Abilities

If you are like most people, you haven't been well coached on how to cope well with adversity, crises, and constant change. This book shows you how to access your inborn survivor qualities and increase your range of responses for coping with whatever comes your way.

This book shows how to:

- Regain stability when your life is knocked off track.

- Cope with unfair developments in an effective way.

- Develop a talent for serendipity.

- Break free from childhood prohibitions that prevent you from coping effectively.

- Increase your self-confidence for handling disruptive changes.

- Avoid reacting like a victim.

- Thrive in a world of nonstop change.

In 1927 a twenty-five-year-old illustrator and one of his older brothers started a cartoon animation studio in southern California. Because they were among the first to master the art of moving picture cartoons, their studio received a big, one-year, renewable contract from a New York film distributor, Charles Mintz. They were to produce a cartoon series named *Oswald the Lucky Rabbit*.

Mintz, who owned the rights to *Oswald*, sent his brother-in-law, George Winkler, to California to watch production activities. Winkler spent many weeks at the studio getting to know the animators and learning production procedures.

When the highly successful first year drew to a close, the illustrator expected to renegotiate a longer, more profitable contract with Mintz. He took his wife with him on a train to New York. The meeting did not go as expected, however. Mintz told the illustrator that he and his brother would have to work for a lower fee if they wanted to renew the contract. The illustrator was shocked and argued that he could not produce the cartoons for less money.

As they argued about the new fee, he discovered that Winkler had persuaded Mintz to take over production of the Oswald cartoons. During the visits to the studios in California, Winkler had secretly arranged to hire away several of the best animators. Mintz and Winkler believed they could cut costs and increase their profits by producing the series themselves. Their strategy in the negotiations was to get the illustrator to give up his right to renew the Oswald contract.

Winkler and Mintz succeeded.

Angry and hurt, the illustrator and his wife, Lillian, left New York and headed home. He had trusted Mintz and Winkler. He had trusted his employees. He had honored his part of the contract and expected fair treatment in return. He had worked many long nights and weekends to meet production deadlines. Now, without warning, the highly successful cartoon series was taken away from him. He would no longer be the producer of the series he worked so hard to develop. His studio had lost its only big account.

Turning Disaster into a Gift

But the young illustrator did not react like a victim to the raw deal pulled on him. During the train ride back to Hollywood, he reflected on his situation and determined that he could create his own cartoon character instead of waiting to be hired to work on other people's ideas.

His first illustration job had been at a commercial art studio housed in an old building in Kansas City. During long hours at the drawing board, he used food crumbs to train a mouse that lived in the building. He called the mouse Mortimer.

What about Mortimer the Mouse as a cartoon character?

Lillian said the name Mortimer sounded too stuffy. This mouse needed a friendlier, more playful name. What about Mickey?

Back at the studio Walt (Disney, if you didn't figure that one out yet) and his brother decided to take advantage of a new technology that added sound to motion pictures. He charged into his new project with enthusiasm. The rest, as they say, is history.

The new cartoon was an immediate success. And Oswald the Rabbit soon disappeared from theaters while Mickey Mouse went on to become one of the greatest cartoon personalities of all time. Instead of reacting like a victim, Walt Disney had converted Mintz and Winkler's unethical conduct and treachery into one of the best things that ever happened to him.

Many successful people have similar, albeit not so dramatic, stories, but they share one thing in common: the survivor personality in action.

Discovering the Survivor Nature

My interest in survivors began in 1953 when I joined the paratroopers. I was sent to Fort Campbell, Kentucky, for basic training and assigned to the 503rd Airborne Infantry Regiment. Part of the 11th Airborne Division, the 503rd had returned from Korea after suffering heavy losses in combat. We were told that only one in ten men had survived.

We heard stories about the 503rd. This was the unit that had parachuted onto Corregidor Island during World War II and recaptured it from the Japanese. These were jungle fighters—tough, unstoppable, and deadly. They would be our training cadre, and we were nervous about what it would be like. Talk about mean, screaming drill sergeants spread through the barracks.

When we started basic training, however, the sergeants and officers were not what we had expected. They were tough but showed patience. They pushed us hard but were tolerant. When a trainee made a mistake, they were more likely to laugh and be amused than to be angry. Either that, or to say bluntly, "In combat you'd be dead now," and walk away.

Combat survivors, it turns out, are more like Alan Alda playing Hawkeye, the mischievous, nonconforming surgeon in the *M**A*S*H television series than they are like the movie character Rambo. A commanding officer of SEALS training at the Naval Special Warfare Center, for example, said in a magazine interview, "The Rambo types are the first to go."

During our training, I noticed that combat survivors have a type of personal radar always on scan. Anything that happens or any noise draws a quick, brief look. They have a relaxed awareness. I began to realize it wasn't just luck or fate that these were the few who came back alive. Something about them as people had tipped the scales in their favor.

They did not exhibit a self-centered "survival of the fittest" attitude. Quite the contrary. They had such strong self-confidence that they didn't have to act mean or tough. They knew what they could do and apparently didn't feel the need to prove anything to anyone. We trainees knew that if we had to go into deadly combat, these were the fighters we'd want to be with.

A Practical Definition

Years later, when I was a graduate student in clinical psychology, I discovered that psychologists and psychiatrists did not seem to know much about the people who hold up well under pressure. After graduation I started a personal research project to understand people with, as I came to call it, survivor personalities. The criteria I developed included those who:

- Have survived a major crisis or challenge.

- Surmounted the crisis through personal effort.

- Emerged from the experience with previously unknown strengths and abilities.

- Afterward find value in the experience.

Using these four criteria as a frame of reference, I listed questions I wanted to have answered.

- How do some survivors of horrible experiences manage to be so happy?

- Is there a basic pattern of personality traits that survivors share? If so, what are the traits?

- Can a person be similar to others with survivor personalities and yet be a unique individual?

- Is the survivor personality inborn or is it learned?

- If it is learned, why do so many people grow up without learning it?

- What percentage of people have survivor personalities?

- What are survivors like when they aren't in crisis? Is there a way to identify such people when things are peaceful?

A Map-Developing Odyssey

One benefit of a good education is learning how to learn. I kept a curious and open mind as I read autobiographies and interviewed hundreds of people over many years—survivors of the World War II Bataan Death March; Jewish survivors of the Nazi Holocaust; ex-POWs and war veterans; survivors of cancer, polio, head injury, and other physically challenging conditions; survivors of earthquakes, tsunamis, hurricanes, and other natural disasters; survivors of rape, abuse, alcoholism, codependency, and addiction; parents of murdered children; and survivors of bankruptcy, job loss, and other major life-disrupting events. I became curious about public employees who remain cheerful and dedicated to their work even while being maligned by the people they serve.

With a quiet mind I absorbed whatever people told me. I allowed the territory to create its own map for me. I gradually began to sense some patterns, some predictable qualities and ways of reacting. I stopped being surprised, for example, to hear survivors laugh at themselves about some stupid thing they did.

I learned that survivors are ordinary people with flaws, worries, and imperfections. When people call them heroes, they disagree. Captain Chesley ("Sully") Sullenberger of US Airways flight 1549, which landed in New York's Hudson River in 2009, downplays his part of the successful landing. He gave large credit to his crew, training, and experience. Media interviews with the crew after the incident showed that they were aware it would take time for them to heal from their ordeal, that they are not superhumans who could resume doing immediately (if ever) exactly what they were doing before. In an interview with Larry King, Captain Sully said, "It's going to take some time to integrate the experience into my persona and get my sleep schedule back to normal." While each individual aboard that plane has had his or her own path to recovery, it was a good sign to see the crew able to make light of their experience when interviewed by David Letterman on *The Late Show*.

It is important to understand, however, that chance and luck are key factors when a group of people is being randomly shot by gunmen, trapped in a sinking boat, or caught in a large burning building. It is as though a cosmic coin toss determined which people would be killed and which ones would not. In every crisis and emergency, however, some people have a better chance of surviving. If you are still alive after a major catastrophe, there can be a small window of time when what you do can make a difference.

I learned that a few people are born with their survivor traits firmly intact. They are the natural athletes in the game of life and have a natural talent for coping well. The rest of us need to work consciously to develop our abilities. Just as we would have to take lessons and practice to become musicians or artists, we have to work at learning how to handle pressure, difficult people, negative situations, and disruptive change.

I learned that some of life's best survivors grew up in horrible family situations and that many people least skillful at coping with life's difficulties have come from ideal homes. Many of the strongest people in our world have been through experiences that no public school would be allowed to arrange. They have been strengthened in the school of life. They have been abused, lied to, deceived, robbed, raped, mistreated, and hit by the worst that life can throw at them. Their reaction is to pick themselves up, learn important lessons, set positive goals, and rebuild their lives.

I learned that people seldom tap into their deepest strengths and abilities until forced to do so by a major adversity. As Julius Segal, a distinguished survivor researcher, has said, "In a remarkable number of cases, those who have suffered and prevail find that after their ordeal they begin to operate at a higher level than ever before. . . . The terrible experiences of our lives, despite the pain they bring, may become our redemption."

For example, former POW Lieutenant Commander Charlie Plumb was kept in an eight-foot by eight-foot stone cell for six years. He had no window to look out and nothing to read. He was frequently hog-tied, beaten, and subjected to grueling interrogations. Now, when he talks about his experience as a POW, he says, "It's probably the most valuable six years of my life. Amazing what a little adversity can teach a person. . . . I really felt there was some meaning to that, to my experience itself."

Thriving Versus Being a Victim

Again and again you can find stories of people who say their life-threatening ordeals were the most valuable experiences of their lives. At the other extreme, some people who are healthy, employed, and living in safe communities with loving families complain about their lives as though they were being tortured.

The contrasts in people's reactions emphasize that the way we interact with life events determines how well we survive and thrive. Our attitudes determine our well-being more than our circumstances. Some people thrive in the very same situation that is distressing and overwhelming to others. In recent years, thousands of people have lost their jobs through no fault of their own. Many become discouraged and financially distressed, while others find their strengths, start successful small businesses, and are thriving.

Fortunately, almost every person is born with the ability to learn how to handle unfair situations and disturbing experiences. The fact is that anyone can learn how to become better at handling life's challenges. It is possible to avoid victim/blaming reactions by developing learning/coping responses.

A Teaching Challenge for Me, a Learning Challenge for You

Years of observing and learning about life's best survivors have convinced me that:

- Survivor qualities can be learned, but they can't be taught.

- Survivor qualities and a survivor spirit develop out of everyday habits that increase chances of survival should it become necessary.

- People trained to act, think, and feel as instructed do not cope with life's unexpected challenges as well as a person with self-developed abilities because life's best survivors have each developed a way of coping that is unique to them.

A frustrating situation for a teacher! How can I teach what can't be taught? How can I offer expert advice about surviving and thriving when people who try to do what an expert says may, in fact, lower their chances of coping well with unexpected difficulties?

My way of handling this challenge is to offer coaching tips on how to manage your own learning. If you've read many self-help books, you may have noticed that the authors often start by saying that none of the existing self-help books worked very well for them. It was only after they compiled their own list of habits or principles that they finally found the way to greatness, effectiveness, excellence, prosperity, wealth, love, power, spirituality, or good digestion. Their book, they say, will save you the time and struggle of reading any other books.

The effectiveness or workability of any plan, however, comes from the learning struggle. In the school of life the responsibility is on the learner, not the teacher. Through trial and error you learn what works and what doesn't work for you. True self-improvement, self-confidence, and spiritual development come out of real life, everyday experiences, not from books or workshops.

Thus my approach is to provide guidelines on how to learn

your own surviving, coping, and thriving skills. This is a book of useful questions and practical guidelines. It is not a book of instructions. Think of it as a manual on how to discover inborn abilities that no other human can reveal to you.

What We Will Cover

Curiosity is one of the most important survivor qualities. When you ask questions about how things work, you acquire practical knowledge you can use in new situations.

The world of work has changed drastically. Many employees now work without job descriptions as members of self-directed teams. Chapters 2 through 6 cover what it takes to cope and thrive in a world of constant change—without an authority telling you what to do. These chapters show how the ability to thrive comes from ways of feeling, thinking, and acting that parents and teachers have typically not encouraged in children, including guidelines that show you how to embrace people with negative attitudes.

Many chapters contain explanations of the psychological principles involved. Feel free to skip those parts if you want only the guidelines for handling a specific situation, but realize that your learning should not be limited to one or another unique

Self-Development Suggestion

At various places in the book you will come across a suggestion in a box like this one. If you want to get the most out of the book, take time to do the suggested activity. In addition, *The Survivor Personality Manual*, a workbook, is available through www.THRIVEnet.com.

occasion. Understanding the underlying principles will always serve you well. If you understand how the psychological principles of cause and effect work, you can apply the ideas to a wide variety of new, unexpected situations.

The best survivors are those who find a way to convert misfortune into good luck. Chapter 7 explains why a talent for serendipity is a primary indicator of a survivor personality and how you can develop yours.

The biggest challenge for most people trying to cope with difficult situations is breaking free from inner prohibitions that act as invisible emotional handicaps. Most children are born with the inner motivation to learn how to survive and thrive, but something happens to them during childhood. The natural process of self-motivated learning is disrupted when parents and teachers try to turn boys and girls into "good boys" and "good girls." This phenomenon is examined in Chapter 8.

The escalating pace of life has created numerous challenges facing many people today—too much pressure, too much change, negative people, angry people, and events that have an effect on our lives and livelihoods that are seemingly well beyond our personal control. Chapters 9 and 10 contain specific guidelines for handling difficult situations in ways that make you stronger. In each case, the coping effort shows how to thrive by converting the difficulties into valuable personal growth. (If you are trying to cope with an extremely difficult situation right now, go directly to Chapter 9.)

What about life-and-death situations? Chapters 11 and 12 offer insight into what others have done when thrown into the worst possible circumstances. While there is no prescription for survival in crises, disasters, and torturous conditions, we can learn from the experience of others, as Julius Segal suggests in his book *Winning Life's Toughest Battles*. The value in learning about many kinds of survival is that one person's way of surviving cancer, for example, may carry just the right clue for someone struggling with months of unemployment.

There is no way of existing on this planet that does not have its drawbacks. Chapter 13 provides insight into some of the difficulties survivors encounter because they are survivors, and tips for how to handle them.

And finally, Chapter 14 gives you tools for creating a self-managed learning plan for developing your own palette of surviving and thriving skills.

Friedrich Wilhelm Nietzsche, as quoted in Victor Frankl's *Man's Search for Meaning*, said, "That which does not kill me, makes me stronger." *The Survivor Personality* shows you how to do just that. It shows how to cope with disruptive change, tap into the will to survive, and gain strength from adversity. It shows how to convert a distressing, unfair experience into something good for you.

TWO

Playful Curiosity
Learning What No One Can Teach

Most introductory psychology textbooks define learning as a relatively permanent change in behavior that results from experience. In a world that is constantly changing, it is important to understand that change requires learning. The two concepts, *change* and *learning*, are inseparably linked.

The kind of learning that leads to thriving is self-managed learning directly from experience. It is the kind of learning that young children do when they play. To play is to learn—nature's way.

Learning How Things Work:
Experimenting with Life

Playing and experimenting are linked to human survival. Human infants are not born with the same ability to survive on their own as the young of other animals. Humans need more time to learn how to care for themselves than do members of other species. The noteworthy principle here is that the more the young of a species are born ready to survive on their own, the less they can learn later in life.

Maria Montessori, internationally recognized as an outstanding educator of children, said that a child's playing "is effortful, and leads him to acquire the new powers which will be needed for his future."

Years ago, psychologist Robert W. White explained in "Motivation Reconsidered: The Concept of Competence," an article in *The Psychological Review*, that because "so little is innately provided" to humans, "much has to be learned about dealing with the environment." What is called child's play "involves discovering the effects he can have on the environment and the effect the environment will have on him. To the extent that these results are preserved by learning, they build up an increased competence in dealing with the environment."

How Humans Learn What They Can Do

Each person's growth and development is influenced by three different kinds of learning. One is the inner, self-motivated, self-managed learning that comes directly from *experience*; learning that results from the urge to explore and play.

Another kind of learning occurs from imitating those around us. Through *modeling*, we acquire the action patterns of others.

A third kind of learning is controlled and *directed by others*. Unfortunately, too much training and instructing by teachers and parents pull a child away from his or her inborn capacity for self-managed learning. This is why some students passively sit in their chairs waiting to be taught and why some employees passively wait to be told what to do. That is how they were raised.

They became conditioned to let others give them instructions on what to think, feel, and do.

Locking a child into a prescribed way of acting, thinking, feeling, and talking early in life may make things comfortable for the adults raising him or her, but the child then becomes like an animal born with predetermined behavioral patterns—it is blocked from self-managed learning and changing later in life. In a rapidly changing world, a person stuck in a fixed pattern is less able to adapt.

It is important to understand that a child's inborn predisposition to ask questions tends to be suppressed rather than encouraged by adults. Think back to when you were a child. Were you praised for pestering your parents with questions? Did teachers thank you when you interrupted the lesson they were teaching with questions about something else? Probably not. Have you ever been to a high school commencement where a graduating senior was honored for being the best student in the class at asking questions?

In most homes and schools, asking questions is not viewed as a skill or talent to be cultivated, not nearly as much as learning answers. This is the case even though life's best survivors ask lots of questions—good questions, impudent questions, disruptive questions.

People who adapt and thrive are like curious, playful children who never grow up. They retain from childhood a curiosity about what exists. They love learning how things work and may become delighted, laugh, and grab anyone nearby to show them. Such people often approach something that attracts them in a playful way. For them, playfulness is the way to learn how things work. They enjoy playing with situations, people, and their own experiences.

The life-long child asks: How does this work? What is that? What if I did such and such? What would happen if I acted in another way? What if I tried something different?

Discovering Cause-and-Effect Relationships

Experimenting and playing show a person the relationship between what she did and what happened as a result. Having experienced this relationship, she may repeat the action to confirm that the same outcome occurs. Or she may try a variation to observe if the outcome changes.

Experimenting leads to firsthand knowledge of relationships between events. If such and such is done, then certain outcomes usually occur. If, for example, a boss tries to take credit for the crew working hard to meet a deadline, then the workers may not work as hard next time there is a crunch. Experimenting enables a person to see for herself what will happen. To experiment is to learn from your own experience.

Playful people putter, tinker, or just plain fool around. Author Robert Fulghum writes in his book *All I Really Need to Know I Learned in Kindergarten* about how he likes to sort clothes when they come out of the dryer because "there's lots of static electricity, and you can hang socks all over your body and they will stick there." Once, when his wife discovered him covered with warm socks, he says, "she gave me THAT LOOK. You can't always explain everything you do to everybody, you know."

Curiosity can lead a person to find out what she can get away with. When told about a particular rule, she may break it just to see what will happen. Sometimes such people conduct secret experiments. Someone might have an affair, for example, just to find out what it is like. Playful people may appear to be wasting their time, but their playing leads to learning about themselves and the world.

Becoming Competent

Solutions we discover for ourselves frequently work better than those that others give us. Life's best survivors are not especially bothered when what they see and think does not fit with the way that others think. They will experiment with different ideas or points of view to find out what works best. They seem less interested in who is right. They are more interested in connections between cause and effect. Furthermore, they continually seek information and new ideas that will explain how things work and how to make things work better.

The really competent people in every sphere of human activity are those individuals who go beyond their teachers. They learn what they are taught, may try imitating what someone else does well, and then continue to learn what no one else could teach them. In contrast, people who follow instructions on how to be successful are seldom as successful as they could be.

Think about several of the most capable people you know. Are they effective primarily because of a class they took or a training program they went through? No. Effectiveness, competence, skillfulness, and mastery result from self-motivated, self-managed learning.

Becoming Life Smart

The psychologists who created IQ tests ran into a problem. The average seventeen- or eighteen-year-old could do as well or better on intelligence tests than could people thirty or forty years old. Try as they would, psychologists could not construct an IQ test in which adults got better scores than high school juniors and seniors. (The psychologists' solution was to engage in a sort of professional slight of hand. They decided to say the average score for each age group would be equal to an IQ of 100. Thus, even though the average eighteen-year-old gets a higher score than the average forty-year-old on the same test, they are both given an IQ score of 100.)

Intelligence tests cannot measure how well a person handles life's challenges. They don't measure smartness. If IQ tests did, an uneducated taxi driver would get a higher score than a professor on how to survive on the streets of a big city. Having a high IQ is much different from being life smart. No recent graduate with a masters in business administration could have assumed the presidency of Apple and brought it back from unprofitability, as Steve Jobs did in 1997, when he returned to the company he founded. In 2009, he was named *Fortune* magazine's CEO of the Decade. That took someone with years of experience.

How do people become smarter and smarter as the years go by? How is it that a person can get better and better decade after decade?

Getting smarter year after year comes from having child-like, playful curiosity, being guided by feelings, and learning from experience. Psychologist Daniel Goleman, author of *Emotional Intelligence*, says this way of interacting with the world is how a person gets into the *flow* that develops emotional intelligence. He says that "flow represents perhaps the ultimate in harnessing the emotions in service of performance and learning."

Getting smarter comes from asking questions and searching for answers, from experimenting with life, and from even being willing to look foolish and make mistakes. Such an orientation to the world and to your experiences enables you to develop an increasingly accurate understanding of your world and leads to increasingly better skills.

How to Learn from Experience

A specialist in vocational rehabilitation once said to me, "In the schools you go to as a child you sit in classes where first you learn the lesson, then you take the test. In the school of life it is the opposite. First you take the test, then you learn the lesson."

He is right. The question is, How does a person or an organization learn from experience? Here are useful guidelines:

- If you are upset, express your feelings. Clear your emotions.

- Reflect on the experience; replay it in your mind as an observer. Avoid explanations that either justify or condemn what happened. You don't learn when you rationalize, justify, or criticize what you have done. (Managers thwart learning when they blame a person or group for mistakes.)

- Describe the experience. Tell a friend. Write about it in a journal.

- Ask yourself what you can learn from the experience. If such a thing were to happen again, what would you do next time?

- Imagine talking or acting in a more effective way next time.

- Rehearse doing it the way you desire.

Take some time to reflect about something difficult that you went through, such as a divorce or a major conflict at work. By following the steps just listed, you can learn about yourself. Trace back to early clues you ignored. Decide what to do and not do the next time. When you process experiences in this way, you will increase your self-confidence for handling similar situations better in the future.

Laughing Goes with Learning

Laughing about something learned is an excellent sign that valuable learning has occurred. Learning that results in personal growth is emotional as well as mental. The kind of learning associated with increasing life competence happens in the body, not just in the mind.

Laughing as a reaction to learning means that healthy emotional education is taking place. Insightful learning, especially about oneself, can be a delightful experience. It stays with you a long time—much longer than information you memorized for a class.

Playfulness and Laughing Are Survival Skills

Captain Hawkeye Pierce, the character played by Alan Alda in the popular television series *M*A*S*H*, was a good example of someone who used his playfulness for emotional survival. Hawkeye knew that as a mobile army surgical hospital surgeon, his primary responsibility was to use his medical skills with the sick and wounded. As a draftee who viewed the Korean War as insanity, he maintained his emotional stability by playing with his circumstances.

In the midst of death and wasted lives, he invented ways to remain playful. He would break military rules but would never violate his professional standards. When the gung-ho doctor, Major Frank Burns, would threaten Hawkeye, Hawkeye would usually laugh and find a way to embarrass the major.

Life-competent people often do that—laugh at threats. They react like a martial arts master might respond to an attack by a child. And their amused laughing may be all it takes. Because they do not respond by feeling threatened, they are able to disarm people looking for a fight.

Playing and laughing go together. Playing keeps you in contact with what is happening around you. A playful spirit lets you maintain an attitude of "This situation is my toy. I'll play with it as I wish." A friend of mine recounted that she went to the hospital with one of her friends who had to have a breast removed because of a malignant tumor. Afterward, as the woman began to recover from the anesthesia, my friend asked, "How are you?" The woman looked down at the bandages on her chest and said, "I'm all right, I still have 'vage.'"

"Your what?" my friend asked.

"They took 'clea,' but I still have 'vage,'" she said, laughing.

My friend told me, "I knew immediately that with a sense of humor like that, she was going to be fine."

Another advantage of playful humor is that it allows you to redefine the situation emotionally. The person who makes humorous observations is relaxed, alert, and focused outward on the situation to be dealt with. Engaging in playful humor may lead to a creative solution.

Benefits of Self-Managed Learning

Curiosity, questions, playing, experimenting, and laughing allow a person to learn valuable lessons from failures and develop new strengths. Carole Hyatt and Linda Gottlieb say that during the research for their book *When Smart People Fail*, they discovered that "almost everyone we talked to, especially the most currently successful people, had experienced some major failure in their past." Their in-depth interviews with 176 successful people showed that "it is the way you cope with failure that shapes you, not the failure itself." They found that most of the people they interviewed were *learners* and concluded, "If we learn from an experience, there can be no such thing as failure."

The benefits you gain from self-managed learning include being able to:

- Read situations and new developments rapidly.

- Handle change well.

- Find a useful lesson in bad experiences and look forward to the next incident with positive, even eager anticipation.

- Build self-confidence and become more willing to take risks. If things do not work out, you will still gain by learning something useful.

- Try guidelines suggested by others to see how well they work for you. Then adapt and modify the guidelines to fit with your style, your situation, and your purposes.

- Develop an increasingly accurate inner mental map of the world around you.

- Get better and better as the years go by. You are a constant learner in the school of life. You become more and more life smart.

- Be the first to adapt or create a new way of doing something. You do not have to wait for others to solve problems and teach you the solutions.

- Learn new ways to be employable or provide a new service or product in a shifting, changing, unstable world.

Learning is a way of life for people best at surviving and thriving. When change is constant, learning is an essential survival skill. Next we will see how learning from experience leads to another essential skill—being flexible.

THREE

Flexibility

An Absolutely Essential Ability

Tough challenges may call on your ability to use both logical reasoning and your intuition. Although these qualities may seem to be contradictory, being able to use both can be a tremendous help in doing the right thing at the right time.

A teenaged Rosyann sat before me one day and told me about her parents getting divorced when she was five and how her father kidnapped her after school one day. She had been with him in California for almost eight years before he was arrested and she was returned to her mother.

Rosyann told me about feeling sad when she left her friends in California, how she handled coming back to live with a mother she barely remembered, and what it was like to come back to a small town in Oregon after living most of her life on the streets of large California cities. When it was time for Rosyann to leave, she paused. She said, "There's one thing that puzzles me. . . ."

"What's that?" I asked.

She looked down and fiddled with her shoe. "I know I'm social," she said, keeping her head down. "I like being with people a lot, but sometimes I'm antisocial. I have to get away from people and don't want anyone near me."

She glanced up to check my reaction. I sensed her caution. "Good!" I said. "I'm glad to hear that! It means you are very mentally healthy!"

Her eyes lighted up. She broke into a big grin and said, "Wow! You mean I'm not schizy?"

"No. Just the opposite. You are more mentally healthy than most people. I'm really pleased to hear that you have both kinds of feelings."

"Whew," she said, letting out a big sigh. "I've worried about being a schizo."

"Not at all," I said, "Good survivors like you have all kinds of opposite feelings. You'll notice more as you get older."

This exchange between Rosyann and me had to do with my discovery that life's best survivors sometimes feel like misfits and that a key source of their strength is viewed by some people as emotional instability.

Take a few moments to check off the traits you possess and add any important ones not listed. While much valuable information about survivorship comes from talking with others, many clues lie within you. As a baseline assessment, which of the following traits do you recognize in yourself?

sensitive	tough
strong	gentle
cowardly	courageous
mature	playful

humorous	serious
distant	friendly
self-confident	self-critical
trusting	cautious
dependent	independent
impulsive	well-organized
happy	discontent
cooperative	rebellious
proud	humble
selfish	unselfish
involved	detached
lazy	hardworking
logical	creative
calm	emotional
shy	bold
loving	angry
consistent	unpredictable
messy	neat
optimistic	pessimistic
_____	_____
_____	_____

The Basis for Survivor Flexibility

Survivors puzzled me at first. They are serious and humorous, hardworking and lazy, self-confident and self-critical. They are not one way or the other, they are both one way and the other.

This was a hard mental barrier to break through. Most tests of personality view a person as either one way or another, not both. Popular magazines, for example, often conduct surveys such as "What Makes an Ideal Mate?" asking readers to indicate the qualities of their dream partner. Questionnaires will list pairs of qualities and ask readers to choose between them. They ask questions like: "Is an ideal mate extroverted or introverted?" "Is an ideal mate critical or nonjudgmental?" and "Is an ideal mate self-confident or self-doubting?" Surveys such as this force you to respond to only the choices they present. Often a form returned with "all of the above" or "it depends on the situation" written on it is viewed as invalid and thrown out.

Many authors write about people as being optimists or pessimists, as type A or type B personalities. Yet many survivors are both optimistic and pessimistic, impatient as well as calm. How can a person be both one way and the opposite? What is the relationship between being a survivor and having paradoxical personality traits?

When I ask survivors if there is any quality or trait that contributes most to being a survivor, they usually answer without hesitation either flexibility or adaptability.

But how do you do flexibility? What makes mental and emotional flexibility possible?

We find an answer in the writings of T. C. Schneirla, a scientist famous for his studies of animal behavior, who concluded that for any creature to survive it must be able to move toward food and safety or away from danger. Schneirla described the ability to approach as well as to withdraw as being a "biphasic pattern of adjustment."

Biphasic patterns of movement are possible for us because of opposing muscular systems in our bodies. We have command over our physical actions because our flexor and extensor muscles work against each other in controlled opposition.

Just as we can move our bodies in many different ways because of our opposing muscular systems, we can have contradictory emotions because the sympathetic and parasympathetic nervous systems also work in controlled opposition. The parasympathetic nervous system enables us to respond with relaxed, peaceful contentment, while the sympathetic nervous system enables us to have a fight-or-flight reaction in other situations.

These counterbalanced nervous systems give us a range of different reactions to different circumstances. Because we have two nervous systems working in controlled opposition, we can run toward something in joy or away in fear. Because we can do both, we have some choice over responding in both one way and the other.

Mental and Emotional Flexibility

Physiological principles usually have counterparts in personality. What is true of the body is often reflected in the mind. The equivalent in personality of counterbalanced nervous systems and muscle systems are oppositional traits of personality—the paradoxical qualities—that enable an individual to respond in both one way and another.

Biphasic personality traits increase survivability by allowing a person to be one way or its opposite in any situation or to fall anywhere along the continuum in between the two extremes. To have biphasic traits is to be more adaptable rather than being either one way or another. It is to be proud and humble, selfish and unselfish, cooperative and rebellious.

Response Choices

Pairs of biphasic, paradoxical, or counterbalanced traits are essential to a survivor style because they give you choices about how to respond. Look back at the checklist. See how many pairs you checked off. The more pairs of traits you recognized in yourself, the more likely it is you have survivor qualities. If you added other items to the list, that's even better. The list is not meant to be complete. It never could be. The list is presented to demonstrate the biphasic principle.

People who hold up well in what I call crossfire jobs usually have many paradoxical qualities. Head nurses, for example, must handle emergencies; demands from patients, administrators, physicians, patients' families, and insurance companies; and the needs of many hospital departments while conforming to laws governing all the ward activities.

Employees in today's world of constant change must respond in different ways to different demands. To respond in the same fixed way to all situations reduces your ability to adapt to changing events and circumstances. The ability to respond in a variety of ways gives you choices and makes you much more adaptable—even though having biphasic qualities may feel strange.

Why Is Flexibility So Vital?

The important thing is having many such pairs of opposing traits, whatever they may be. The longer the list of pairs of paradoxical or biphasic traits descriptive of you, the more complex you are and, typically, the better you are at successfully dealing with any situation that develops. The people involved in my survivor personality research project agree that being flexible and adaptable are central to a survivor personality.

Why does having a complex personality increase your survival chances? Having a variety of available responses is crucial when handling variable, unpredictable, chaotic, or changing conditions. Successful people in any profession know that it is better to have many possible responses than to be limited to a few.

Adaptation is the key to survival in nature as well as among people. Two biologists, Lorus J. Milne and Margery Milne, commented on successful patterns of survival in the animal and plant kingdom:

> The plants and animals that survive in their progeny are the lucky ones. They hold the winning combination: a successful pattern fitting one place and time, and the ability to modify the pattern in the correct direction as fast as the environment changes. The luckiest of all have an adaptation ready, still unused, as though prepared for alteration that has not yet come. They gain a head start in the altered world. Less fortunate are those whose pattern limits them to a single situation. They vanish forever.

Aron Ralston, a rock climber who in 2003 found himself pinned by an eight-hundred-pound boulder, says he quickly realized that he had four choices: be found, chip away at the boulder, move the boulder, or cut off his arm. For him, dying wasn't an option. After six days and lost hope on the first three plans (and even accepting his own death), he ended up amputating his own arm. Aron says that during his ordeal he experienced the whole range of emotions and mental states. He says he would have arguments with himself about cutting off his arm. His self-talk ranged from optimistic to pessimistic, but eventually he was able to do what he needed to do to rescue himself.

The One-Way Mistake

If you look at someone who does not handle life well, it is often because he always thinks, feels, or acts in only one way and would never consider the opposite. Many people are so taken with the idea of being self-starting, for example, they lose sight of the need for the counterbalancing skill of being self-stopping.

A person who can only act in one way has little self-control and therefore must be kept in check by external forces. Take, for example, someone who doesn't know when to stop talking. Such a person keeps going and will continue until the listener terminates the conversation. The less a person can consciously follow his favored pattern, the more he feels helpless and controlled by external forces.

Many college students act as though they had only two choices about studying. At one extreme is the bookworm and at the other extreme is the party animal. Students who get the most out of college, however, are able to both study and play. They study effectively, stop, and then have time for other important activities.

A salesman asked me about why he would have periods of many days when he was not able to make himself do anything. He said when he was on a roll he could go for many hours. His water-filtering device was such a hot item he could go into a cocktail lounge at 1:00 a.m. and sell units to the bartender and several customers. But he'd sometimes run out of energy and couldn't leave his apartment for days.

The problem? He didn't know how to stop himself, take a break, and rest. His body would protect itself and take control at a level stronger than his willpower.

In resiliency workshops for managers, I often have participants get into small groups and list the qualities of the best and the worst manager they've ever known. When the groups read their lists, it is clear that an effective manager is very flexible. Such a person adapts well. Excellent managers are both people oriented and focused on results. They are both friendly and task driven.

The point here is that the old way of thinking was that your personality traits were constant in all situations. The new way of thinking is that your traits are a function of how you are choosing to interact with the situation you are in.

On work teams, for example, a fluid, adaptable person might be the informal leader when things are in turmoil or be a quiet follower if things are running well. He might be the creative brainstormer when the group is stuck or the conservative voice of caution if others are trying too many new ideas. If the group is overly optimistic, this person might be pessimistic but then optimistic if the group is too pessimistic.

A more effective way to view people, and one that allows

better understanding, is to assume that every person is more complex, unpredictable, and unique than any label. To assume a person is more complex than any theory opens up the possibility that a person can be both one way and the opposite.

By describing what people feel, think, and do with adverbs and adjectives instead of labeling them with a noun, when they change from one situation to the next, we can be comfortable with their shift instead of getting upset when they don't stay consistent with the way we have them categorized. For example, if you think of a person as a "pessimist," you leave little room for that person to be able to step outside of the perceived label and act in any sort of optimistic way—at least in your mind. Instead, describe the person as behaving pessimistically when they do pessimistic things. This way it is much easier to allow for them to also be optimistic at times. Recognizing the flexible traits in others will help you develop your own.

Developing Emotional Flexibility

If being more emotionally flexible seems desirable, a practical question to ask is, How does a person develop these biphasic or paradoxical abilities that seem so important to flexibility and thus to survival?

For adults, the course of development depends on one's starting point. For example, if you dislike conflict, your developmental path is to learn how to be firm and confrontive.

Such an undertaking is difficult, however, and it will take years of practice. Why so? Developing a counterbalancing ability often requires acting in ways you have ridiculed or condemned in others. A person raised never to get angry usually has negative perceptions of people who express anger. If you are forceful and competitive, then conciliatory people are seen as wishy-washy scaredy-cats.

One-way perceptions, regardless of content, are examples of polarized thinking in which we feel repugnance for our disliked opposites, for our anti-models. That is why, when an unassertive person is urged to learn assertiveness, her reaction is usually, "I couldn't do that." For her to be assertive would be to act like a despised authoritarian.

Similarly, when a fear-inducing, tough-acting person is told to be more appreciative or to be a good listener, the inner reaction is no. For an autocratic person to listen well, express sincere appreciation, and be influenced by subordinates would be to act like a despised, weak, gutless person who gets shoved around.

Emotional aversions to your anti-models run deep in the subconscious and are not easy to overcome. It takes a combination of frustration and courage to become more paradoxical—frustration when your habitual approach doesn't work well in important situations and courage to see that what you previously despised in others may have some merit. We will go into this process in more depth in Chapters 8 and 9. For now, however, we need to look at another barrier to being a person with paradoxical qualities.

It Isn't Easy Being Multifaceted

Moshe Feldenkrais, the renowned originator of body movement techniques that foster better physical integration, observed in his book *Awareness Through Movement* that "reversibility is the mark of voluntary movement." An action that cannot be reversed is involuntary. It is reflexive and is not under conscious control. If you always respond one way and never in the opposite way, you will sometimes be helpless to stop yourself from reflexively doing or saying something that you'll later regret.

Look back to the checklist of traits you filled out earlier in the chapter. Just by reading about the benefits of having counterbalanced traits and a flexible nature, and by not being confined to "either/or" constructs, how many other traits on the list can you now check off?

Learning About Positive and Negative Attitudes

Becoming flexible includes developing attitudes that seem counterintuitive. One of life's great irritations is having to associate with people who complain all the time. It wears on your nerves to be around a constantly negative coworker or family member. It hurts when they criticize your suggestions and see nothing good in your plans. It might not be so bad if the person considered your suggestion carefully, evaluated its merits, and then pointed out deficiencies. What is irritating is that people with negative attitudes react with an unthinking, pessimistic reflex.

Does it work to try to make such people change their attitude? No. They reject your efforts to get them to see things in your more positive way. Your efforts to perform an attitude transplant have no chance of success if the recipients are unreceptive.

Can anything be done? Yes, once you understand the source of the problem, a solution emerges.

The first few times I gave a workshop called "How to Keep a Positive Attitude in Negative Situations," I decided to find out what the people in the workshops thought about the differences between someone with a positive attitude and someone with a negative attitude. I put them into small groups and had them list the differences.

The following list is just a sampling of what most people typically come up with:

POSITIVE ATTITUDE	NEGATIVE ATTITUDE
friendly	unpleasant
cheerful, smiling	frowns, sulks
open-minded	closed-minded
accepts others	blames others
optimistic	pessimistic
helpful	makes excuses
humorous	whines
good listener	uncommunicative
constructive	finds faults
enjoys work	complains

Who Is Negative?

Something about the two lists puzzled me. The descriptions seemed out of balance. Take a moment to see if you can spot what it is. Pay special attention to the emotional tone of each list. The descriptions in the two lists express a belief that being positive is much more desirable than being negative. The positive list reads almost like a funeral eulogy. It includes statements that people identify with and often use to describe themselves. The negative list contains words we use for people who irritate us.

What the two lists show is that most people with positive attitudes have a negative attitude about people with negative attitudes!

An Emotional Handicap

The belief that positive thinking is desirable and negative thinking is undesirable is a version of the child's good person–bad person personality theory (see more about the good-child handicap in Chapter 8). If your way of thinking about positive and negative people is similar to the two lists, you know that your belief feels right. But the drawback is that reacting to a disliked opposite in negative ways renders you helpless with such a person. It is emotionally handicapping.

Why so? For a combination of reasons. First, because perception is based on contrasts, you are using the negative (bad) person as a frame of reference for your positive (good) person identity. Second, you believe that for things to improve, the negative person should change instead of you. Third, you spend lots of time and energy in unsuccessful efforts to try to make him not be the person your good person identity needs for him to be.

These reasons help explain why in most families, organizations, and work groups, a person with a negative attitude has the most power. In your mind you have it set up that unless the other person changes, the situation will never improve. You have placed your fate in the hands of another person and then blame him for not being willing to change. You empower his negative thinking and then want him to give up his power.

It is not uncommon for workshop participants to confess, "I

came to your workshop because I've always been such a positive person, but my . . ." At this point the rest of the person's statement is pretty predictable as he points out that his partner or child or coworker is someone who is always negative.

When a positive-attitude person has a negative attitude about negative attitudes, somewhere in that person's world there is a negative person who makes life difficult for him. It's a sure bet, because that is how the laws of nature function. The clincher is that he is operating from a good-child identity when he claims that he is acting only for the other person's own good.

If your lists describing positive and negative attitudes are similar to the lists given earlier, it shows that you were taught a rigid way of thinking that is emotionally handicapping. Your strict attitude toward negative people makes it possible for negative people to have much more control over situations than you do. By being negative, they can upset you, cause you to spend time and energy trying to cope with their negativism, and frustrate your efforts.

What can be done? First, recognize that your distress, frustration, and lack of success are signs that you do not understand what is going on. Second, stop your victim/blaming thinking: "If only he would change, my life would be much better." Third, shift to the curious, empathetic, flexible mode of thinking that makes a person a survivor. Find out what is valid about a person who repeats a negative mental/emotional pattern over and over.

Oftentimes people with negative attitudes derive benefits such as gaining attention (albeit negative), not having to hide their feelings, avoiding responsibility for bad outcomes, and being left alone. You can deal with some of these energy-draining people by avoiding them, withholding attention from them, asking them to be considerate of your time or attention, asking them to also see something positive, making their complaint seem more extreme than it really is, or simply viewing their complaining as an adult form of crying—and brush it off. Tactics for dealing with people you can't avoid include having them clarify what outcome they are looking for, point out all the difficulties they see that you might encounter, or put their grievances or bad predictions in writing—so they can either cool off before they approach you or you can track the outcomes to their predictions to see if their negativity is valid or not.

Many people with opposing or counterbalanced personality traits have been told there is something wrong with them. People with rigid thinking can't handle complex or negative people very well, and often view them as defective. Women, in general, have more paradoxical traits than men and thus have more survivor personality traits.

Questions to Strengthen Your Flexible Thinking

Is being paradoxical something you are comfortable with?

When you were growing up, were you allowed to be inconsistent in your thoughts, feelings, and actions?

Were you instructed to think, act, or feel in one way only? What happened when you had inconsistent feelings or thoughts?

When someone you know acts, feels, or thinks in contradictory ways, do you stay relaxed? Tolerant of their inconsistencies?

From your knowledge of survivors, can you verify the paradoxical or biphasic traits in them?

Can you consider having a positive attitude about negative people?

One summer I was teaching a workshop called "Indicators of Psychological Fitness" at a health education conference. I had taught the same workshop the year before and recognized some of the participants. I asked why they chose to attend my session again. A woman in her midtwenties said, "Last year I learned in your workshop that I wasn't schizophrenic. You helped me see that it is healthy, not sick, to have two opposite feelings." She paused, stared into my eyes, and added "I needed that. You'll never know how much I needed that. I came back to learn more this year."

A few weeks later, a woman took me aside after I finished giving a talk about the survivor personality to her professional women's group. She shook my hand with vigor and said, "Thank you! You've cured me of my mental illness."

WE come now to some new questions: How are some unpredictable, paradoxical, shape-shifting people able to be highly effective while other unpredictable people are draining to be near? What gives paradoxical people a sense of direction? How do they know what to do in situations they have never faced before? How do they know what not to do? And, if having paradoxical traits provides options about ways to respond, what determines their choices?

Answers to these questions can be found by examining a strong motive in life's best survivors: the need to have things work well.

FOUR

The Synergy Imperative
Needing to Have Things Work Well

THE best survivors are good troubleshooters. They are handy. They are inventive. They often come up with remarkably easy solutions to difficult problems because they want and need for things to work smoothly and easily.

A good friend told me of a story often repeated in Japan about one of its largest soap manufacturing companies. They received a complaint from a consumer who had purchased a box of soap that was empty. An internal investigation revealed that once in a while, for reasons the company engineers could not explain, this had happened.

While management worked on a long-term fix, a group of engineers was told to devise a way to prevent any empty boxes from being shipped out. They worked quickly to create an expensive, hi-tech, scanning device that would spot the occasional empty box. Their hurriedly assembled device didn't work right, however, causing a big inconvenience in the production area.

Meanwhile, one of the line workers took it upon himself to rig up a temporary solution while the engineers worked at perfecting their scanning equipment. He placed an electric fan near the conveyer belt where the sealed boxes came out. Any empty soap boxes passing in front of the fan were simply blown off the line.

Needing for Things to Work Well

The need to have things work well explains much about why some people are better survivors than others. The need for good synergy is a central, motivational principle in their lives. This motivation helps explain why they have common sense and, when necessary, can succeed in a situation that no other person has ever faced.

Their sense of knowing when things are working well and when they are not doesn't come from following rules or memorized techniques. It comes from an inner awareness or feeling about nature's laws and principles. They have a good sense of what Mihaly Csikszentmihalyi calls "flow" in his book *Flow: The Psychology of the Optimal Experience*. When things are not working well, these people do not complain; instead, they feel an urge to make improvements.

When things are working well, life's best survivors tend to drift into the background of events. They may appear to be lazy or inattentive, but this is not the case. Their attitude is typically something like this: Why should a person spend energy when it isn't necessary? They do not have to show off their strengths. They do not need to manipulate events to try to claim credit for successes. When things are working well, they understand that intruding into the actions of others would be disruptive and energy draining. Interference for personal gain causes a waste of human energy, time, and resources and disturbs people who like to have things work well.

At work, they may seem to have soft, easy jobs. That is often true. Their jobs are easier because they worked very hard to get things that way. Somehow when they are around, meetings run more smoothly, people work together better, equipment runs efficiently, and work is done more pleasantly.

Synergistic Humans

Ruth Benedict, a cultural anthropologist, is credited as the first person to use the word *synergy* as a way to describe human activities. She used the term to explain differences she had observed in the quality of life between one culture and another. Benedict's ideas are applicable to groups as well as cultures. High synergy exists in an organization when minimum effort results in cooperative and effective action. Low synergy exists when it takes excessive effort to get even routine matters done.

Trying to get something done in a low-synergy organization is like driving a heavily loaded truck and trailer down the highway when all the tires are flat. Working in a high-synergy organization is like cruising along the highway in a new sports car.

High synergy helps explain why some self-directed work teams get better results than could be predicted from looking at the individual members. A group of good workers can combine their talents to create an outstanding team. The synergy comes from the positive interaction of the different individuals to create results beyond what any team member could produce alone.

Low-synergy groups produce less in the way of results than

would be predicted from looking at the individuals. This can happen when managers are unethical, egotistic, overly autocratic, or lack basic management skills.

Synergy is the outcome of how individuals interact.

The Synergistic Personality

People with survivor personalities could also be described as having synergistic personalities. The term used for describing the way the person interacts with the world is not important. It is the same personality style.

The link between the survivor nature and being a competent, synergistic person is as follows—when things are working well, such a person:

- Sits back and lets things run themselves.

- Expends less energy than people who are struggling.

- Has periods of optional time for detecting the early signs of new developments.

- Devotes attention to the little things that count.

- Spots early indications of potential trouble and takes action to prevent it.

- Prepares for future events so that when they occur things fall into place easily.

- Is more relaxed, happy, and views working as a stimulating activity.

- Puts high-quality time and energy into emergency developments without having other basic matters interrupted.

- Acts in ethical ways even when no one could catch them cheating.

- Responds to an emergency or crisis with an attitudinal reflex of both expecting and needing for things to work out well.

The Need for Good Synergy Is a Selfish Need

People in whom the synergy motive is strong volunteer to help when there is trouble. People with survivor personalities are foul-weather friends. When things are working well, they may seem to be uninvolved; but when there is trouble, they show up, ready to lend a hand or take charge.

They do this, in part, because when others are in pain, they feel it strongly. When things are going well for others, they feel better. Their effort to eliminate a problem or reduce pain or distress in another person has a selfish component.

The need for good synergy is a selfish motive because the better integrated a person's thoughts, feelings, and actions become, the more the person needs a pleasantly functioning world in which to live. Being exposed to discordant, unstabilizing, energy-draining, disruptive people or conditions can be painful. In his book *The Revolt of the Masses*, the Spanish philosopher José Ortega y Gasset wrote, "Contrary to what is usually thought, it is the man of excellence, and not the common man, who lives in essential servitude."

The need for good synergy in people who are good survivors is paradoxical, because they make the world a better place for themselves by devoting themselves to making it better for others. They are both selfish and selfless at the same time. They have resolved what Abraham Maslow called the "selfish-unselfish dichotomy." They have achieved a state of selfish altruism.

Maslow stated:

In highly developed, psychiatrically healthy people, self-actualizing people, whichever you choose to call them, you will find, if you try to rate them, that they are extraordinarily unselfish in some ways, and yet also they are extraordinarily selfish in other ways. . . .

High synergy from this point of view can represent a transcending of the dichotomizing, a fusion of the opposites into a single concept.

In other words, synergistic individuals act unselfishly for selfish reasons. They must, for their own good, take action to improve discordant, energy-draining situations. Actions that result in things working better lead to feelings of satisfaction and may be profitable as well. The two are not incompatible.

Anthony Robbins, famous for his inspirational speeches, books, and tapes, says, "I am totally and completely focused on delivering to my audience what they really need." In his newsletter "Sharing Ideas," he wrote, "If you are totally sincere, if you really care about people, and give your all, you succeed." By the age of thirty-two, Robbins had the satisfaction of helping thousands of people discover how to improve their lives, and his businesses were bringing in over $50 million a year. He has benefited both emotionally and financially.

Low- and High-Synergy Managers

The synergy concept provides a useful framework for explaining the difference between the effects obtained by those managers with a controlling, autocratic style and the effects obtained by managers who successfully run flatter organizations where teams of people work autonomously. Low synergy results when a boss sets the goals, uses threats, interferes with the way people work, exerts tight control, tries to solve all the problems, and attempts to make people perform well. High synergy results when a manager has everyone participate in goal setting and problem solving and leaves people free to do their jobs as they think best.

Some Disadvantages

Is being synergistic the ideal? Not always. No way of doing things is without its limitations. A former college classmate told me about a problem she had because she was *too* effective! She was a department manager in a state agency. She had developed her people so well and had her department running so efficiently that some upper-level administrators were bothered when they saw such a relaxed, friendly group of workers. They decided her department did not have enough work to do.

She had documented that her department produced more work per person, of higher quality, with fewer errors, and at a faster rate than any comparable unit. But still she heard about upper-level grumbling that her people did not appear to be working hard enough. She later resigned, took her retirement money, and opened a pasta place in a mall. More fun for her, but a great loss to the state.

Becoming More Synergistic

If developing synergistic skills is desirable to you, there are ways to do so. Here are some suggestions:

- Approach new, unstable, or difficult situations with this question in mind: How can I interact with this so that things turn out well for everyone?

- Look for creative ways to help make things work well. Ask others, What would you like to have happen? Volunteer in a way that lets others refuse your help if they wish.

- Recognize and admit that you have selfish reasons for wanting to have things work well for others.

- Don't tell anyone that what you are doing is only for their own good.

- Develop a personal code of moral principles and ethical practices.

- Search for ways to convert difficulties into an opportunity to make things better.

- Realize that it is all right to be successful at what you do and be paid well *without working hard*!

- Learn the difference between *allowing* things to work well and trying to *make* things work well.

- Ask yourself what you are uniquely qualified to do in your current life situation that would be useful for others.

As you gain experience, the habit of looking for ways to interact to have things turn out well becomes reflexive. When potential problems or emergencies arise, you react almost instinctively as you absorb information and act to meet the challenge at hand.

A sign that you have developed a synergistic nature is that you accomplish more with less effort. Your life flows along pleasantly and smoothly. People who are synergistic think not of time management, but of energy management. You get all the important things done and still have spare time to do what you enjoy.

The need for good synergy helps explain why there is no good personality test for the survivor personality. The best assessment of synergistic people is to look at how well things are working around them. Survivor personality traits are determined more by the situation than by fixed inner habits.

Wanting and needing to have things work well for everyone means that you must have an accurate understanding of what other people feel and think. This brings us to a uniquely human survival skill. That skill is empathy.

FIVE

Empathy Is a Survival Skill

I N his book *Surviving the Future*, historian Arnold Toynbee gave this response to a question asking him what advice he would give to the younger generation:

> Try, I would say, above all, to remain compassionate-minded and generous-minded; try to remain capable of entering into other people's states of mind . . . even when you strongly disagree with them. Try to put yourselves in the other people's place and see why they hold these opinions or do these things with which you so strongly disagree.

Empathy Development

Empathy is the ability to comprehend accurately what another human thinks and feels. Empathy can be learned. Being curious, letting in new information, and experiencing feelings enable you to develop an accurate, empathetic sense of what is going on in others.

It is important to distinguish empathy from sympathy. A sympathetic reaction occurs when one person takes on the same feelings as another. When a friend experiences a personal loss and you cry with them, that is sympathy. To empathize is to understand and recognize the feelings of someone else without having the same feelings.

The best survivors read and comprehend what is going on in others. The empathetic reading of another person comes from asking such questions as, How does that person feel? What does she see? What might he do? How does that person experience me? These questions open your mind to understanding another person's needs, fears, views, and so on.

To understand the relationship between empathy and survival, look at people who have been under the domination, threat, or control of others. Women, for example, have managed to survive for centuries in a world in which men have held official power. As a result, women, it seems, have learned how to understand men much better than men have ever understood women. In my corporate seminars, male supervisors and managers have asked, "How can I understand women better?" Never once, however, has a woman asked, "How can I understand men better?"

Empathy Makes Good Business Sense

Empathic understanding can affect organizations both internally and externally. Many administrators and executives confuse sympathy with empathy. Fearful of the consequences of having a sympathetic reaction to workers, they avoid exposure to workers' views and feelings. As a consequence, executives can be placed at a strategic disadvantage when presenting, for example, a new process that turns out to be unpopular or clumsy. Management is stunned when the workers revolt and don't buy in to the new rules. When this happens, managers often lack an understanding of the day-to-day workings of the existing process and fail to get input from the employees using it. When people in authority avoid understanding those who are trying to appeal to them, the power of their authority erodes.

In addition, for groups of workers to be effective as teams, each member must have empathy for the other members, the other teams, and especially the consumer.

In the battle between corporations for sales and market position, the side that best understands the customer has the advantage. As competition has heated up in recent years, sales organizations have had to give up trying to make customers buy the way they want to sell. They have had to sell the way customers want to buy. To survive, they have had to develop more empathy for people they wanted as customers.

Run an Empathy Check on Yourself

Imagine that you are someone who works or lives with you. See how accurately you can describe that person's experience of working or living with you. If you are willing to take a risk, try asking the person you have in mind to listen to your impressions. Ask for feedback on how accurate you are.

Personal Empathy Increases Learning

The ability to absorb what another person thinks and feels lets you benefit from their learning experiences. If you study success-ful people, their learning becomes your learning. Most people who master their profession start with a strong motivation to learn from the best. They mimic the successful methods before slowly integrating them with their own experiences and develop-ing their own style. In the family dynamic, interviews with young-est children will often reveal that they learned from the mistakes made by their older siblings.

This type of empathy allows you to expand your toolbox of survivor responses by recognizing and learning about the possi-ble consequences of different reactions to experiences that you may not have had or considered on your own. If you find your-self in a situation in which someone is telling you something outside of your comfort zone, focus on listening objectively to his story. Regardless of whether you agree with his action or reaction, you can learn from the outcome. Ask yourself, "What would I have done the same? What would I do differently?"

Situational Empathy

Your level of empathy is one indicator of the difference between being intelligent and being street smart. People in control often do not live by the same rules they force on others. Because they have set up systems to help ensure that their own safety is a given, they don't feel the need to be as tuned in to the information that empathy might reveal to them in any given situation. For exam-ple, most people know that during periods of a down economy, property crimes often rise. One recent night, fourteen car break-ins occurred in a high-end suburban neighborhood through which few outsiders pass and where the residents had reported feeling very safe. Police noted that almost all of the luxury vehicles were unlocked. If the people in this neighborhood had better situational empathy—especially during a down economy—they might have considered the reality that thieves can strike anywhere, at anytime, and locked up their valuables.

The best way to enhance your situational empathy is to work on becoming more aware of the world around you. Pay the most attention to people and things that seem out of place. If, for example, you are in a public place or commuting, try not to bury your attention in a book or project so much so that you become oblivious to everything around you. Attempt to keep your awareness at a level that allows you to focus on getting your work done while remaining aware of subtle changes in your situation, such as the boarding of a slightly loud or unruly passenger. It's better to decide to monitor at a low level and choose to ignore a developing change than be caught off guard by it.

Pattern Empathy

Another type of empathy is pattern empathy. Good examples are everywhere. A first-rate football quarterback reads the movements of all other players on the field and has a sense of what they will do. In addition to hours and hours of practicing the plays, such apparently instantaneous comprehension requires taking into account the plan for the present play as well as his knowledge of the outcome of all the previous plays.

A successful orchestra conductor must be able to detect, among dozens of instruments, the one player who is a little slow, soft, or off-key and bring that person into line with the entire group.

Popular playwrights, too, demonstrate an astonishing understanding of the differences among individual personalities as well as how these players interact with each other and in various situations.

In each of these circumstances, a successful person shows a command of pattern empathy—a practical understanding of the relationships between cause and effect; a recognition of what goes with what and what doesn't belong. It is a sense of pattern harmony as well as what causes discord. All of them appreciate the effects of little things and have the ability to predict what will get the best results in the time available. They got this way by recognizing and analyzing the patterns around them and discovering the contribution of each element of the pattern.

Pattern empathy—the comprehension of the complex nature of dynamic relationships—is well developed in those with a survivor personality because such people are able to read the signals and understand the cues. The best sportsmen, musicians, writers, lovers, comedians, therapists, public speakers, teachers, group leaders, parents, stage performers, salespeople, military leaders, and so on know what to do and when to do it.

You can develop your pattern empathy by experimenting with how you interact with the patterns around you. Begin with something you know well and test a new action or hypothesis while noting the outcome. Make just one change at a time and if possible, test each new idea a number of times. Start simply— take a different route home, listen to a different radio station, try a different workout, respond to a coworker in a different way, or change something else you do daily largely out of habit—and move on from there. Not only will you gain an appreciation for cause and effect, you may be exposed to additional options for acting or reacting to any of your current situations. It is through the practice of and experimentation with your ordinary daily circumstances that you develop your own understanding of what may or may not help you through a future extreme event. There is no requirement to adopt any of the changes you make. The point is to learn to recognize that there are multiple possibilities of reacting to any situation and that different reactions can bring about different outcomes.

Spotting Early Clues

People with pattern empathy have a better chance of being survivors because, with minimal clues, they can spot a pattern and pick up on hidden agendas. Norman Locke, a friend who owns a coin company, has done very well over the years because he is street smart. His survival in a business fraught with con artists comes in part from his talent for quickly knowing which people are honest and which ones are trying to cheat him with a confidence game. Norm has three clues he uses to spot the shady characters:

- **Ego.** Con artists often make a comment or joke about what they are up to because they feel contempt for their pigeons. When you ignore that clue, the con artist feels justified in taking you for all she can get.

- **Confusion.** Con artists seek to confuse their victims with lots of extraneous information, complicated procedures, and obscure terms. Most people want to look smart and won't admit they don't understand. This is often the smoke and mirrors that hides the con artists' real agendas.

- **Forced Agreement.** The scammer uses the technique of asking questions that will get a lot of yeses from you—and then she tries to rush you into saying yes to a deal before you feel ready.

Experience with life helps you learn the difference between imaginary fears and early clues that are legitimate warnings of eventual developments. Experience helps you develop a keen eye for the details that make you a competent professional.

Like other survivor qualities, however, there can be a downside to empathy.

A Disadvantage to Empathy

Women taking action to divorce physically abusive husbands often need much emotional support because they know their husbands will feel extreme distress. Compassionate executives forced by economic conditions to discharge workers and close plants often experience great emotional turmoil.

Empathy for other people's feelings requires a counterbalanc-

Run an Empathy Check on Yourself

Think back to a situation in your life that turned out poorly—a job, a relationship with someone, or a business deal. It is quite likely that you had early warning signs about this eventual development, but you chose to ignore them. You did not want to believe the early indications about what might eventually happen. Follow the guidelines for learning from experience given in Chapter 2 and decide what you will do the next time.

ing quality of toughness. The same sensitivity that leads a person with the survivor personality to create conditions in which things work well also makes him vulnerable to other people's distress.

Empathy in Dangerous Situations

Being able to read a situation rapidly, understand the underlying patterns, and have the self-confidence to carry through in any situation are the true hallmarks of the survivor, as clearly demonstrated in Joe DiBello's story:

Joe DiBello strode toward the office tower where he worked with long, fast strides. Lunch had taken longer than he planned, and he had important work to do. He pushed through the entrance doors and, being preoccupied with the work waiting for him upstairs, he recalls, "I was in the middle of the lobby before I realized that one of the handful of people standing in the lobby was this guy in fatigues with an AK-47 assault rifle pointed toward the ceiling." At the same instant he saw several women "standing like deer frozen in headlights."

The man with the rifle yelled at DiBello to stop, but DiBello didn't slow down. "I saw that the gunman was trapped in the lobby. He didn't want to be there." The gunman was unfocused, glancing all around. DiBello yelled to the man, "I don't have time for this," and never broke stride.

The gunman tried to fire several warning shots, but his rifle jammed. By the time he took a handgun from his belt and fired several shots into the air attempting to frighten DiBello into stopping, DiBello was around a corner and out of danger.

DiBello says, "I grew up on the East coast. The only way to get personal space in the city is to ignore the crazies in your path. I decided to not recognize him as an authority, not to give him the power. I would have relinquished my freedom and independence if I broke stride, so I kept moving."

The gunman shot and wounded two people before giving himself up to police a few hours later. Was DiBello stupid? Foolhardy? No. His quick, empathetic, accurate reading of the gunman and his own self-confidence let him retain control of the situation while he removed himself from danger. Some might call him selfish, but entering into the situation unexpectedly, he knew there was nothing he could do to assist the others, so he saved himself.

IN survival situations, empathy and the need to have things work out well allow a person to function at a level of spontaneous effectiveness that can be amazing. The key is to understand that subtle emotional components can provide valuable, even though seemingly irrational, inner guidance. Other qualities with emotional dimensions that can lead to surviving, thriving, and serendipity are intuition, creativity, and imagination.

SIX

The Survivor's Edge

The Subconscious Resources of Intuition, Creativity, and Imagination

A VICE president of a chain of theaters told me about an incident that happened when he was having dinner at the home of one of his newer theater managers. The manager was in his midtwenties, married, and had two children. He was a charming, talkative host.

Partway through the evening the vice president had a wholly unexpected flash of insight: *This guy is ripping me off!* He continued to be a pleasant guest for the rest of the evening, but the next day, he had the corporate controller search the theater's records for signs of embezzlement. "Sure enough," he said, "we found it. The manager had discovered a way to skim money out of snack bar sales."

The conscious mind is like the tip of an iceberg floating on top of a much larger subconscious mind. People who have a good relationship with subconscious processes—hunches, intuition, dreams and daydreams, creativity, imagination, and synchronicity—have an advantage over people who try to be only logical and rational.

Intuition as a Survival Skill

Psychologist Weston Agor, founder of the Global Intuition Network, says that intuitive managers "function best in crises or situations of rapid change." He reports in a *Business Horizons* article, "How Top Executives Use Their Intuition to Make Important Decisions," that, "without exception, top managers in every organization differ significantly in their ability to use intuition to make decisions on the job." In his book *The Intuitive Manager*, Roy Rowan describes intuition as "knowledge gained without rational thought." Some people have unexplainable intuitive flashes, others develop intuition by practicing. In either case, intuition is the ability to be receptive to information coming through one's subconscious mind.

Demystifying Intuition

Your brain has much more subconscious information swirling through it than can ever be grasped by your conscious mind. Did you know that one of the main functions of the nervous system is to block conscious awareness of all the stimulations hitting our sense receptors? A stimulus must reach a certain level of intensity before you become conscious of it. Notice in the following illustration how conscious awareness remains at zero until a stimulus builds up to an intensity strong enough to reach the threshold level, called the *limen*, by psychologists.

Limen is the Latin word for "threshold." Research into the

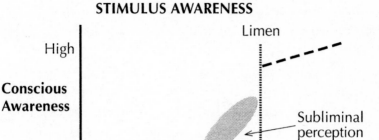

way thresholds work has revealed that the body begins to respond in detectable ways when stimulation is at a level just below this threshold or sublimen. Instruments like the ones used in lie detector tests show that the person's body is registering awareness of the stimulus even when the person has no conscious awareness of it. The facts are indisputable: every human is physiologically equipped for subliminal perception.

Research on the subliminal included the famous experiment in which messages to buy popcorn are flashed on a motion picture screen during a movie. To the dismay of the theater owner, what was subliminal for the average person was above the threshold for the more sensitive person. Some people complained and demanded their money back. But flashing the message faster to make it undetectable to the most sensitive people dropped it below the subliminal level for most of the audience. The small increase in popcorn sales did not cover the cost of the equipment.

Research shows that people have different threshold levels for subliminal perception. Also, a person's sensitivity can change, depending on his alertness and physical condition. The point here is that some people are better survivors than others in part because awareness of subtle reactions in their bodies gives them useful information.

With practice, anyone can improve his ability to access subliminal information. For example, when someone is talking to you, her tone of voice and body language may be out of harmony with the words she says. Once you notice your body is responding to something, even though you are not consciously aware of what that something is, you can lower your threshold of consciousness by relaxing and being curious about what is happening. Your overall survivor orientation—how you perceive the cues and clues around you—is enhanced by being sensitive to subtle inner feelings.

Once alerted, the survivor reaction is to remain focused on discovering what is up. The person attentive to subliminal cues may choose to continue on as though unsuspecting, like the vice president of the theater chain, or may stop and ask questions about what is going on. In either case, the person remains alert and curious about what is really occurring.

Monitor Your Physical Response

The next time you are in a meeting or are discussing an important matter with someone you do not know well, scan your body once in a while. A tight stomach, breathing fast, a hand clenched into a fist under the table, a bouncing foot, or a slight feeling of agitation may be clues that something is not quite right. These signals can be set off by anything—a person's tone of voice, something not said, a group's quietness, a forced laugh, someone's quick glance—anything that does not fit.

Letting Your Body Protect You

Many survivors report that they take action without understanding why or having logical reasons for what they do. For example, a student nurse told me about the following incident:

> Last spring, I was sitting at the bus stop down on Sixth Avenue, waiting for the 3:40 bus. It is the one I usually take up the hill to school. The sun was shining for a change, and I sat on the bench enjoying it. The warmth felt good after days of cold, wet rain.
>
> I still do not know why, but I stood up and walked back to stand near the wall of the store on the corner. I didn't want to be in the shade, I wanted to be in the sun, but I stood there anyway. Something was holding me there. It felt weird.
>
> A few seconds later, a car came racing up the hill. It was a teenage boy in a souped-up car with big tires. When he came around the corner, he lost control and skidded across the street. The car bounced up over the curb and smashed into the bench right where I had been sitting. I couldn't believe it! I still do not know why I got up and moved.

Is this an example of extrasensory perception? Probably not. At some level of consciousness her past observations would have taught her that cars coming up the hill around that corner often have difficulty making the turn. Since she moved only a few seconds before the car hit, it is more likely that in her relaxed state she subliminally detected the sound of the speeding car when it was several blocks away.

Many people are survivors because they have acted on hunches even though the actions didn't make sense. Also, when no logical solution is apparent, an individual with the survivor orientation can operate on feeling alone.

People with intuitive abilities allow themselves to experience whatever they feel. They let themselves react to people and situations as children do. They do not apologize for their feelings. They may decide, for practical reasons, to not reveal a feeling, but that is different from allowing rational thinking to squelch intuitive impressions.

Led by an Inner Guide

Some people survive because of an exceptional ability to trust subconscious directions. Winston Churchill was a war correspondent when he was a young man. While in South Africa covering the Boer War between South Africa and England, he was captured and sent to prison in Pretoria. One night he managed to escape. Emerging from the prison, though, his problems were far from over. As he describes it, he walked out alone into the night and assessed his situation. Three hundred miles stretched between him and safety. He could not speak Dutch or Kaffir, the two languages of the region. The towns and countryside were heavily patrolled, roads guarded, and trains searched. He wondered, "How am I to get food or direction?"

Winston managed to get aboard a train carrying empty coal sacks and rode most of the night. Before dawn he jumped out of the train and hid. During that day, he says, "I prayed long and earnestly for help and guidance." When night came, he struggled on foot over rough country, through scrub bushes, bogs, swamps, and streams. Drenched, exhausted, weak from hunger, and almost drained of hope, he saw some distant lights and struggled toward them. He approached but then hesitated. What to do?

"Suddenly, without the slightest reason," he said, "all my doubts disappeared. It was certainly by no process of logic that they were dispelled. I just felt quite clear that I would go. I had sometimes, in former years, held a 'Planchette' pencil (akin to using a Ouija board) and written while others touched my wrist or hand. I acted in exactly the same unconscious manner now."

He walked to the distant fires and came to a coal mine with some houses grouped around it. He had heard that a few English residents were still in the country to keep the mines working. Had he been led to one of these?

He approached a two-story stone house and knocked on the door. The man who answered was English. Winston identified himself and told of his escape. The man said, "Thank God you have come here! It is the only house for 20 miles where you would not have been handed over. But we are all British here, and we will see you through."

They hid Winston in a chamber at the bottom of the mine for several days. They arranged an escape route for him, and he eventually made his way to freedom.

People with a survivor style follow hunches and use intuition as a natural part of their lives. Author and outdoorsman Robert Godfrey described Outward Bound instructors in his book *Outward Bound: Schools of the Possible*:

The best Outward Bound instructors are those who have the ability to trust their own intuitive responses most faithfully and to act on the basis of those intuitions. It is a real act of personal faith for the instructor to respond to his or her own convictions in the Outward Bound situation, where both the physical and psychological welfare of the participants are at stake.

Godfrey said that when he watched one particular instructor deal with a challenge:

> She doesn't mentally reach for the instructor's handbook. She doesn't flip through the rules and regulations and guidelines to find what somebody else says she should do to deal with the situation. What she does do—and you can literally see her do it—is first and foremost *compose herself*. Her eyes just ever so slightly glaze over, not the glaze of a daydreamer, but the intent expression of a person looking inward, a deliberate closing out of peripheral and distracting stimuli. . . . It is clear that her attention is temporarily inward, checking out her internal response to what is happening.

Developing Intuition

Developing intuition as a reliable, trustworthy skill is a matter of practice. First, begin with deciding to be more receptive to subconscious, irrational information even if it is contrary to what seems logical.

Second, plan ahead. The next time you are in a situation in which there is some confusion or you have to make a decision without all the facts, detach your conscious mind from the external action. Relax. Stop inner conversations. Scan internally for answers to these silent questions: What am I feeling? How am I reacting? What is happening? What would be the best action to take?

Third, keep a record. Whether you acted on your impression

or not, write down what thoughts, impressions, or feelings you got from your subconscious. Then check later to see how accurate you were.

Just observe your results. Do not try too hard, and avoid criticizing yourself if you are off target or make an inaccurate call. Critical, judgmental thinking suppresses intuition.

Programming Intuitive Actions

Some people program their subconscious minds to provide guidance for survival. Harold Sherman, author of several books on ESP including *How to Make ESP Work for You*, says that after several close calls in New York traffic, he decided to instruct his mind to always give him guidance. He says he put himself into a relaxed, meditative state and instructed his subconscious "In the event I should be faced with an accident, to instantly, by impulse, do the right thing to protect myself."

Some months later he was riding in a cab when he said he received a strong urge to move immediately to the other side: "I had no sooner done this than the cab driver shot across Fifth Avenue going against the lights! In that instant, I saw we were going to be hit by an old truck, which subsequently was found to have been filled with lead pipes."

"My first impulse," Sherman says, "was to grab the strap which hung beside the car door and to brace myself for the coming impact, but as I took hold of it an inner voice commanded, 'Let go of that strap!' From that moment on, something inside me took over, causing me to put my arms across my face and head and double up my knees to protect my body."

The truck hit the cab broadside with such force the cab flew through the air, landed on its roof and turned over twice before coming to rest. Sherman says that when he was lifted from the cab, spectators were amazed that anyone could have come out of that taxi alive. Later, when interviewed by an insurance adjuster, Sherman learned that he had instinctively done the right thing. The adjuster explained that most passengers in accidents grab for the straps. This makes their bodies rigid, and, as a result, they suffer broken bones, head and internal injuries.

Many such examples make it clear that intuition is not a random, mysterious human experience. It is a useful ability that can be developed and cultivated like any other.

Television star Carol Burnett escaped injury during the big 1994 earthquake in Los Angeles because she trusted her intuition. In an interview with Charles Grodin on CNBC, she recounted how she woke up about 3:00 a.m. the day of the earthquake feeling agitated. "I got out of bed," she said, "and walked around my house. I could feel that something was about to happen. I suspected it would be an earthquake. I can always tell when there will be a big one."

She went back to bed, but instead of lying down on the side where she always sleeps—the side with her night table, lamp, telephone, and the remote control for her television set—she got on the other side. She said, "I lay there knowing an earthquake was coming. I wondered if I should get up and stand under a door frame, but decided not to."

Things got very quiet. She said she felt a deep silence. She pulled her covers up and covered her head with a pillow. Thirty seconds later the earthquake hit. "My house and bed shook violently," she said. "I felt something fly over me and hit the bed. When the shaking stopped, I peeked out from under my pillow. My bedroom furniture looked like it had been thrown around and knocked over by a poltergeist." Her eyes widened as she said, "I looked at the other side of the bed. The earthquake had hurled my big TV set out of its cabinet onto the side of the bed where I always sleep."

What Did That Dream Mean?

The most direct access to the subconscious mind is through dreams. When we fall asleep, our rational, logical thinking relaxes. Our brains take a break from doing what we want and do what they want. Research shows that every person dreams and that dreaming is essential to maintaining an integrated personality.

Our dreams contain information about what is happening in our lives, our bodies, and the world around us. But the language of dreams takes time to learn and understand. For a person receptive to subconscious information, however, being curious about what a dream might have meant can lead to fascinating insights.

Some dreams are so obvious it takes no special effort to understand, but others take some work. According to Gillian Holloway, author of *Dreaming Insights: A 5-Step Plan for Discovering the Meaning in Your Dream*, learning how to discover meaning in your dreams starts with making the effort to remember and record your dreams. Develop the habit of asking, during the first moments of awakening, What did I dream last night? Then observe what you recall. Holloway says, "Tag the dream with a key word or phrase that identifies the dream. This helps you remember the dream later when you want to record it."

To examine a dream for its meaning, write it down as soon as you can. Then ask, What did this dream mean? To make sense of what seems to be nonsense ask, What is my impression of what this means? What was my feeling in the dream? Is this feeling

similar to any situation in my life? When you practice remembering, recording, and examining your dreams, you improve your
intuition skills. You increase your ability to catch creative solutions that swim by in your thinking like fish in a river.

Creativity as a Survival Skill

While intuition is a matter of listening to your subconscious,
creativity is a matter of coaching your subconscious to bring you
a solution or idea. Psychologists define creativity as an unusual
idea or action that works right.

In difficult or dangerous situations, survival solutions and
actions must often be creative. This story of Lieutenant Colonel
Iceal Hambleton, whose airplane was shot down in Vietnam in
1972, is a perfect illustration. Wounded in the attack, Hambleton
parachuted into an area controlled by the North Vietnamese.
Although he had radio contact with the U.S. planes above, the
helicopters could not get in to rescue him. With little food or
water, after seven days Hambleton was getting perilously weak.

Aerial photos showed that he could escape by following a
narrow, complex route, but since the North Vietnamese military
was listening to the radio transmissions between Hambleton
and the planes above, the pilots could not tell him what route to
take.

At command headquarters they brainstormed ways to get
him out and came up with a creative plan. Hambleton was an
expert navigator and one of the best golfers in the air force—
with a quirk. He knew the exact length and compass directions
of all the holes on his favorite golf courses.

On the ninth night Hambleton heard the pilot flying above
tell him to get ready "to play a brisk eighteen holes." The first

hole was to be hole number one at the Tucson National Golf Course. Hambleton looked at his map. They wanted him to walk 430 yards southeast.

When he reached "the first green," a clump of brush near an abandoned village, he reported in. The pilot above congratulated him and said the next hole would be hole number five at Davis Monthan Air Force Base. That meant they wanted him to walk 100 yards east. Next was hole number five at Shaw Air Force Base, and so on.

This brilliantly creative solution allowed Hambleton to escape from extremely dangerous territory. It took him four very difficult nights, but he eventually reached a rendezvous point with two rangers who then took him to a rescue helicopter.

This same creative approach to dealing with crises can be seen almost daily in the business world. For example, Tom, a specialist with a large electronics company, reported that one year his company had a serious loss of revenue. As a result, a decision was made to lay off 20 percent of the workforce, which included his job.

Most of the long-time employees felt outraged. Severance pay and outplacement help did not keep morale from dropping. But Tom looked at the big picture. He recognized that he had specialized skills essential to the completion of an important new product. So when he heard that the company would hire a few consultants for essential work, he presented his qualifications to the HR department. They hired him as a consultant to replace himself!

Ironically, a year later the company determined it would save money by hiring Tom full-time instead of paying his consultant fees.

The ability to invent a workable solution to a problem comes from wanting to find a good solution; thinking independently; and stepping outside the boundaries of old perceptions, explanations, and responses. Creativity comes from being able to imagine something that is new and different and yet has the right ingredients. It means being able to allow your subconscious mind to come up with an unusual solution to the challenge at hand.

Research by psychologists shows that creative people—original

Challenge Your Creativity

Creativity comes from the ability to see unusual connections, find unusual ways to combine things, and make remote associations. The following items are patterned after a test of creativity developed by psychologist Sarnoff Mednick as presented in his book *Examiner's Manual, Remote Associates Test: College and Adult Forms 1 and 2*.

Find a word that these three words have in common:

Stool

Powder

Ball

The answer is *foot*—footstool, foot powder, football. Now find the common word for each set of these three words:

1. Blue	cake	cottage
2. Made	cuff	left
3. Motion	poke	down
4. Wood	liquor	luck
5. Key	wall	precious

thinkers—have a perceptual or observational way of looking at the world. In contrast, people lowest in creativity have a judgmental or dogmatic style.

The observing, perceptual person experiences the world with a silent mind. She is open-minded or, if you will, open-brained and absorbs information about how things work just for the sake of knowing. Then if a problem develops and a solution is needed, she has a wide range of information to draw on.

On the other hand, the judgmental style is revealed in such statements as, "Don't bother me with facts; my mind is already made up." People with this style react emotionally and judge others and situations quickly. Hasty judgments shut the mind to information that could contradict their prejudgments, or prejudices. Psychologists describe this mental reaction as "premature perceptual closure." It's a kind of thinking incompatible with creativity. You cannot hope to be creative if facts, details, and information are never absorbed in the first place.

Speeding Up the Creative Process

Brainstorming is a way to accelerate creative thinking. Alex Osborne, originator of the classic brainstorming technique, emphasized in his book *Your Creative Power* that critical evaluation of ideas must be suspended during the idea-gathering phase. Judgmental thinking inhibits the expression or even the thinking of delightful new ideas. The brainstorming process begins with the group involved in choosing a particular problem or unusual challenge and following these guiding principles:

- Take time away from other distractions to make a long list of wild, playful, weird, crazy, uncensored ideas. A good indicator that this is going well—bursts of laughter, groans, and an excited, rapid flow of ideas.

- During the idea-gathering phase, there is to be no criticizing, ruling out, or declaring an idea to be impossible or impractical.

- Avoid evaluating ideas the same day, which could stifle the flow of more suggestions that will come during the evening and the next morning.

- Use critical reasoning to select the two or three best possibilities to evaluate in detail.

Studies of the brainstorming process show that great ideas often come after a period of the uninhibited expression of wild, outrageous, or seemingly ridiculous suggestions. In other words, a really good new idea cannot be reached by going in a logical, straight-line way from where you are to where you think you want to be.*

Imagination as a Survival Skill

In 1937 Howard Stephenson wrote a book, *They Sold Themselves*, about people who were successful at finding employment during the devastating economic depression in the 1930s. He said that the successful job seekers, "the ones who did not have a brother-in-law who could hire them to sweep out the storeroom, all had imagination." He said imagination is only the first step,

---

*For more information about Alex Osborne's ideas on brainstorming, see www .CreativeEducationFoundation.org.

however. The Depression-era survivors that he profiled in his book also had nerve and tact.

The imagination of most survivors is well developed. When I surveyed self-identified survivors and asked, "Would you say you have an active imagination?" they invariably answered yes. Some added such comments as:

> "Unbelievable, and daydream—have done so all my life—do it to the point of not hearing what is around me—it's deeper than daydream, though—it is beyond conscious thought and I did it even as a child."

> "Active is a conservative term."

> "Yes, a dreamer—love to arrange and set up for work and play in my mind."

> "Some days too active."

Imagination has many dimensions. It is a bridge between the conscious and the subconscious mind. It may be a fantasy place where you go to have fun. It may be passive daydreaming. It may be an active and purposeful mental activity in which you brainstorm or interview yourself using a question-and-answer dialogue.

Active Imagining

There is another aspect to imagination that often plays a role in getting things to turn out well. It is the ability to consciously hold an image in your mind, repeat it over and over, and have things turn out as you imagined. This practice is emphasized by all who believe in the power of prayer or the power of positive thinking.

Emile Coué, originator of the saying "Day by day, in every way, I am getting better and better," explained that it is "the education of the imagination that must be sought for." (See Chapter 10 for Coué's idea on how self-talk can be overdone.)

The principle here is consistent with an observation made to me by a minister. He said, "I wish I could make several members of my congregation understand that constantly worrying about something that might happen is the same as praying for it to happen."

What this all means is that your imagination and expectations can work for you or against you. Some people are so creative with their fears about horrible things that might happen, they become paranoid.

A Mysterious Factor: Synchronicity

Life's best survivors accept meaningful coincidences as part of the way the world works. They do not dismiss some related events as occurring only by chance just because they can't explain how such things happen. Carl Jung used the term *synchronicity* in his assertions that there is a causal factor underlying some meaningfully related events.

My experience has me agreeing with Jung about causal factors leading to synchronous events. While I was writing the first draft of this book, for example, I witnessed many of the activities before and after the eruption of Mount St. Helens. At that time, I had not yet started on my research on human nature and Mother Nature. I'd been writing for almost two years and was growing tired of long hours in the library. I thought, "There has to be a current research publication about human behavior in natural disasters. I don't want to go do all the library research myself. There has to be an up-to-date publication about the current perspectives. I wonder how . . . ?"

Two days later I received a phone call from a man who identified himself as Chris Glenn. "I got your name from a friend of yours," he said. "I just got my PhD in psychology and have moved to Portland. I'd like to talk with you about how to get started in practice here."

When Chris told me he had a professional article published recently, I asked him what it was about. "It is a survey of the current literature on natural disasters and human behavior."

TAKEN all together, intuition, creativity, imagination, and synchronicity can give you an advantage in any new, challenging, or dangerous situation. It is comforting to know you can count on your subconscious mind to alert you to danger, provide useful information, or deliver creative solutions. Nonjudgmental receptivity lets you accept subtle feelings, unusual ideas, and useful coincidences.

A paradoxical nature allows almost any thought, feeling or action to be available and gives you exceptional response flexibility. Playfulness and self-confidence lead to appropriate risk taking, experimenting, rapid learning, and making quick corrections. Empathy lets you comprehend what others think and feel. And all these abilities are organized by the commitment to find a way to have things work well for everyone.

Once you have become aware of and develop these abilities, you will begin to notice new ways to turn your obstacles into opportunities and develop your talent for serendipity.

SEVEN

The Serendipity Talent
Turning Misfortune into Good Luck

THE English writer Horace Walpole coined a word for the ability to convert what could be a disaster into good fortune. He named the talent "serendipity." His idea for the term came from his memory of an old Persian story he read during childhood: "Peregrinations of the Three Sons of the King of Serendip."

The story is about three princes banished from their homeland by their father, King Giaffer. Each had received the best possible education, but their father knew they needed to be seasoned by real life. He used a trivial incident as an excuse to become furious at them. He had the princes thrown out with no servants, no horses, no jewels, or money.

In their various adventures together, the three princes used their powers of observation and deduction to make difficult circumstances turn out well. As fairy tales usually go, so goes this one; each eventually married well, became emperor of his own kingdom, and reconciled with the king.

Serendipity is not good luck and is more than coincidence. It is, according to Walpole, an ability in which keen perception is used to convert an accident into good fortune. According to Walpole, three elements must be present to qualify as an example of serendipity: (1) Something accidental must happen, (2) in response to which a person uses his or her good sense or wisdom (3) to discover a beneficial outcome. It turns out that Walpole's childhood memory of an English translation of a German translation of an Italian translation of the Persian story did not accurately reflect the original. But, of course, this turned out to be a serendipitous distortion allowing him to describe his finding.

I've learned that the best indicator someone has a survivor personality is when they talk about their worst experience and then add, "It was one of the best things that ever happened to me."

The Good Luck of Misfortune

The well-known story of cancer survivor and bicyclist Lance Armstrong, multiple winner of the Tour de France, demonstrates many survivor personality traits and ends with a perfect example of making good out of bad. Lance maintains his cancer was the best thing that ever happened to him. Before his diagnosis, he was a self-admitted slacker, not living up to his own potential. During his treatment, he became actively involved in learning about possible therapies and ultimately rebelled against his doctor's initial advice by choosing an alternative chemotherapy cocktail mix that would have a lesser effect on his lungs. It was a wise choice because he may not have been able to return to biking otherwise. He also showed determination and drive to beat his illness. Lance states, "The surest way to get me to do something is tell me I can't." This determination served him long after his diagnosis and recovery. Lance says, "I wouldn't have won even a single Tour de France without the lesson of illness. What it teaches is this: pain is temporary. Quitting lasts forever." Along the way, his ordeal opened his eyes to a much bigger world than cycling. In addition to winning an unprecedented seven consecutive tours, he is now a top fund- and awareness-raiser for wellness and cancer research.*

You Never Know

Imagine renting a rustic wooden cabin in a beautiful forest setting for your honeymoon. The place is delightful. At dawn, however, a woodpecker starts its loud *rat-a-tat* pounding on the roof. The noise is so loud you can't sleep. It happens at dawn the second morning, again on the third morning, and so forth. What would you do?

Many people say they'd shoot the bird. Some say, "Who cares? It's your honeymoon."

This incident with a woodpecker happened to Gracie and Walter Lantz on their honeymoon. They were a happy, playful couple, and they discovered an opportunity. By the time they had returned from their honeymoon, they were inspired to create the cartoon character Woody the Woodpecker. Walter was the illustrator, Gracie the voice. When interviewed on the NBC *Today Show* on their fiftieth wedding anniversary, Gracie said, "It was the best thing that ever happened to us."

Many valuable scientific discoveries have been made serendipitously. Wilhelm Roentgen noticed that radiations passing through an object left an image on unexposed photographic

---

*For cancer survivor information, see www.LiveStrong.org.

negatives. This led to his discovery of x-rays. Arthur Fleming's discovery of penicillin came from noticing a fungus killing the bacteria in some laboratory culture dishes. Even chocolate-chip cookies were discovered by accident.

Finding Serendipity Is Not by Chance

When misfortune strikes, life's best survivors not only cope well, they often turn a potential disaster into a lucky development. How they do it is not a mystery, they follow a general set of steps that you can also follow. When you sense something is wrong:

- Trust your intuition.

- Read and adapt to the new reality quickly.

- React to bad news with questions.

- Find an amusing benefit to the situation.

- Have empathy for all other parties.

- Retain your self-confidence (see Chapter 10) and be tough.

- Search for a way to make things work out well for everyone.

- Look for how to turn disaster into a stroke of good luck.

Look for Serendipity in Your Past

When you think about one of the most difficult experiences in your life, do you see value in it? Do you feel that you gained or benefited in some way from what happened? Can you find the gift? When telling others about one of your roughest experiences, do you mention why it was good for you?

If not, spend some time taking a close look at past difficulties and distressing experiences. Have you ever lost your job through no fault of your own? Had to live or work with a very negative person? Had to deal with angry people? Been forced to cope with a distressing, disruptive life change?

Explore these experiences with questions such as:

- Did I learn something useful?

- Did I gain new strengths? Develop more self-confidence? Become more understanding of others?

- Why can I be thankful that I had that experience? Why was it good for me?

In addition, you can learn about serendipity from asking survivors that you admire these questions. Think of people you know who have been through incredibly difficult experiences and who handle life well, are upbeat, and playful. These may be combat veterans, survivors of childhood sexual abuse, survivors of severe injuries, and so on. Make sure to ask why they aren't bitter, considering what they experienced.

The Serendipity Personality

Life's best survivors are better than most people at quickly turning a disruptive event or adversity into a desirable development. Their reaction to almost anything that happens is "Good! I'm glad this happened! Let's play with this!" If distressed by an unexpected crisis, they do not let themselves feel victimized. They can go from being emotionally upset to coping to thriving to serendipity with amazing speed.

I could have selected the phrase *serendipity personality* instead of *survivor personality* to describe my findings because in my mind they are interchangeable. The better one understands how the serendipity talent is integrated into the survivor style, the easier it is to appreciate why life's best survivors spend less time working at survival than others.

Simple Steps to Creating Serendipity

The talent for landing on your feet comes from habits you can develop by following some simple but not always easy guidelines:

- **Learn to welcome adversity.** There is an old saying that "Good mariners are not made on calm seas." Adversity and misfortune can be catalysts for discovering astounding strength of character. Extreme tests can bring out your deepest strengths if you keep repeating "Somehow, someway I am going to handle this and make things turn out well." The more extreme the difficulty, the greater the eventual benefit.

    When caught off guard by bad news or misfortune, one of the best ways to focus your energy is to remind yourself of your natural ability to pull through. People responding to survivor personality surveys report that when knocked off balance they frequently repeat sayings to themselves, common sayings such as:

    When the going gets tough, the tough get going.

    Every dark cloud has a silver lining.

When life hands you lemons, make lemonade.

When trouble comes in the door, a blessing comes in the window.

- **Laugh or cry.** Laughter is great for getting you more relaxed. If you can't laugh, then cry. One way or another, calm you emotions. Your mind will work more effectively when strong feelings aren't welling up to override your ability to think. Do whatever you must to regain emotional balance quickly.

- **Ask survival/coping questions.** What would be useful for me to do right now? What is the new reality?

- **Be playful and curious.** Toy with the crisis. Poke fun at it. Experiment with your perspective. What are other people thinking and feeling about this situation? Ask serendipity questions such as:

  Why is it good that this happened? Is there an opportunity here that did not exist before?

  How did I get myself into this anyway? (Not said in a self-blaming way, but in a curious, observing way that looks for cause and effect.) Next time what will I do differently?

  What am I learning from this?

  What could I do to turn this around and have it turn out well for all of us?

- **Take action.** Do something different, anything that might in some way lead to a good outcome. Remember: when what you are doing isn't working, try something else!

The Outcome

People hit by adversity or misfortune react in different ways. Some go numb. Some become very emotional in ways that solve nothing. Some become victims. They feel ruined by the misfortune and complain "if only that hadn't happened, my life would have been better."

Life's best survivors react to a disruptive change forced on them as though it is a change they desired. The same crises or disruptive changes that make some people victims are turned into good fortune by people with the serendipity talent.

Interfering with Nature's Plan

Unfortunately, many people were not allowed to develop their survivor traits as children. Most children are born with the inner potential to be survivors, but parents and teachers can sometimes interfere with their development. Children are often trained to stop asking questions and learn only what they are told. They are taught to have some feelings and not others. Many times their intuitions are negated or invalidated.

It is as if the original equipment comes from the manufacturer with a factory-installed software program designed to constantly upgrade itself with use. But well-intentioned parents and teachers who believe they have to train children to feel, think, and act in certain ways interfere with the installed program. They freeze it up so it never develops beyond a primitive level.

As a result, many adults live their entire lives trying to act like "good" boys and girls. The rigid rules of behavior they were taught actually decrease their survivor chances in today's world.

If you find yourself struggling to embrace your full potential, the next chapter shows how, why, and what you can do to break free from such childhood prohibitions. If you already have a sense of your inner paradoxical survival traits, the next chapter will explain why some others act the way they do.

EIGHT

The Good-Child Handicap

A MAN in a dark blue suit walked up to me during the social hour before his professional group's dinner meeting. He introduced himself and said, "You're a psychologist, what can I do to stop my three-year-old daughter from being selfish?"

"In what way is she selfish?" I asked.

"Last Saturday," he said, "some friends came over to our home for the afternoon. They brought their little boy. She didn't want him to play with some of her toys. We told her to share the toys and not be selfish, but she still tried to hold on to her favorites. She cried and got upset when we made her hand them to him."

"What's wrong with her not wanting to let another child play with her favorite toys?" I asked. "Maybe she's afraid something will get broken."

"That's selfish!" he said. "We don't want her to be selfish when she grows up."

*   *   *

MOST parents want their children to grow up to be decent, well liked, and responsible. They do not want their children to turn out bad. But a child's desire to please and become a *good child*, unfortunately, can result in an adult who is unable to cope well with life. Furthermore, such a person can be an energy-draining pain for others to live and work with.

The biggest barrier to developing a survivor personality comes from having been raised to be a good [noun]. For example, in my workshops, when I describe the benefits of paradoxical traits such as selfish–unselfishness or pessimistic–optimism, some people shake their heads and say that I'm asking them to do what bad people do. They resist the idea that being paradoxical might be a source of strength for them. If you relate to this sort of unease, your resistance may stem from inner prohibitions that your well-intentioned parents trained into you when you were a child. These inner prohibitions were often paired with an inflexible style of parenting in which your parents always expected the same behavior from you in every situation.

Parents must watch their children, of course, to make sure they're safe—to stop them from playing with matches or guns. But when parents overprotect and impose extreme restrictions on their children's ways of behaving, their children become like animals born with predetermined behavioral patterns.

Parents who raise children not to be bad, erroneously think they must prohibit all traces of bad ways of feeling, thinking, and acting. They use bad people as anti-models and try to raise their children to be the opposite. Everyone knows about people who cause problems and drain energy from others when they complain all the time, hurt others, act in highly selfish ways, lie, cheat, steal, feel and act superior to everyone else, refuse to cooperate, and so on.

Parents such as the man who asked me how to stop his daughter from being selfish are using prohibitionist logic: by prohibiting bad behavior, you will eliminate all the problems it causes.

In a similar fashion, many parents believe that by prohibiting their children from showing negative, angry, selfish, and rebellious behaviors they will raise a good child. These parents often discourage their child from expressing emotions and asking questions that could lead him to come to a greater cause-and-effect understanding of himself and the situation causing his distress.

When parents and other adults raising a child dwell on what a good child is not, these are the sorts of generic good boy/good girl messages a child hears:

- Don't talk back.

- Be polite.

- Be good.

- Stop pouting.

- Don't whine.

- Don't be angry.

- Don't hit.

- Don't fight.

- Don't be selfish.

- Tell the truth.

- Stop complaining.

- Smile.

- Don't cry.

- Stop asking questions.

Many of the prohibitions appear as *don'ts*. The don'ts are often accompanied by statements of what a good child should feel, think, and do. It is as though there were a rule book for thoughts and feelings that each generation feels compelled to pass on to the next. What are some other statements you heard as a child?

Because perception always requires contrasts, most parents point out to their children what bad boys and girls are like. Typically, a child may hear that bad children are noisy, dirty, or selfish and that they fight, swear, cheat, sass back, skip school, steal, cause trouble, argue, break things, and don't obey their parents.

Children hear these statements about what a good boy or girl shouldn't do, and learn that it is extremely important to cooperate in trying to be good and not to be bad. Being good means getting love, hugs, acceptance, and candy from others. Being bad means getting punished, spanked, rejected, scolded, and sent to your room without dessert. Thus to please their parents and receive much needed love and acceptance, most children try hard to be good and not bad. But there is a serious flaw in the outcome. People raised to be good and not bad can be emotionally handicapped outside the structured environment they were raised in. They are trapped into only good ways of acting and paralyzed from bad ways of acting, even if one of those perceived bad actions could save their life. Because each situation you come across is unique, you handicap yourself if you draw from only a small set of so-called acceptable responses. If you are a parent, you can brainstorm with your child about possible actions and outcomes and the appropriateness of each in a given situation.

A Testimonial from a Former POW

The good-child syndrome is so pervasive in our society that it prevents most people from coping well with rapid change, unexpected difficulties, and extreme crises. When Bill Garleb, an ex-prisoner-of-war, read an early description of the good-child pattern, he immediately wrote me:

> My need to comment is so strong I could not pass it up. When I went to parochial school, as a child, if you changed your mind and could see the other side of something, they accused you of being inconsistent, or "thinking like a woman." In other words, they programmed you to be polarized and one-sided, the opposite of what a survivor personality needs to be to cope. I am overjoyed that I have learned that being biphasic is good. I like myself better now. It is important to note that, although I was trained and programmed as a child not to use biphasic traits, when my survival was threatened, I relied on basic, inborn traits and ignored conditioning.

To survive as an adult, Garleb had to go against how he was raised. His experience is not unusual among survivors.

The Energy-Draining Effect
of Overly Good People

While most people naturally break free from restrictive child-hood patterns in their late teens and early twenties when leaving their parents' home or educational setting, many adults live their entire lives attempting to behave like good children. People raised with lasting inner childhood prohibitions can cause many problems for others. In middle age they still think and act like the child they were conditioned to be at age five.

In general, most good-child traits are welcomed and add to a peaceful, respectful society when they are sincere. Problems occur, however, when people display them while being dishonest with themselves. Not only have these good people not developed the emotional self-awareness and flexibility to be able to handle today's pressures, they drain energy out of others. They may hinder your efforts to enhance or heal yourself. They can be such a pain to live and work with for the following reasons:

- **They do not give you useful feedback.** Even when you ask them to express their feelings directly to you instead of talking behind your back, they won't. While it may be obvious to you that they feel angry or upset, they often cannot admit that they are. If they do admit to being upset, they have a victim reaction. They blame you for causing them to have the unhappy feelings they experience. If you were supposed to telephone and did not, you may be told, "You really hurt me when you didn't call."

- **They are self-deceptive.** They believe their efforts to help others are completely unselfish. For example, when a woman asked me for advice on how to get her husband to stop being so negative, I asked, "Why are you working so hard to change him?"

  "It's for his own good," she said. "He would be so much happier."

  The nature of the good person's self-deception is such that she can act in ways harmful to you, while truly believing she is doing so for your own good. The combination of sweetness in your presence, destructive criticism behind your back, and a belief that her actions are for your own good is behind the statement "With friends like these, who needs enemies?"

- **Their efforts to make others have only good feelings about them often cause the opposite reaction to occur.** For example, if someone tries to force you to eat some candy or cake and senses some irritation or resistance in your attitude, he may work even harder to get the reassurance from you that he wants. His efforts may cause an even stronger negative reaction in you, which leads the person to try even harder—and so on. Instead of doing something different when their actions do not work, they do more of what elicited the negative reaction in the first place. The pity of it all is that they have not learned they would be more likable if they stopped trying so hard to be liked.

- **There is a hidden threat under their efforts to make you see them as good.** If you react negatively to their ways of trying to control what others think and feel about them, they may decide you are a bad person and punish you. The dynamic is this: *Victims need victimizers; victimizers deserve to be punished.* This is why you run the risk of becoming a target for their destructive gossip and emotional abuse if you do not let them coerce you into expressing only those feelings for them that they need to hear.

• **They avoid empathy.** They become slippery when you try to discuss an upsetting incident with them. In their way of thinking, some things they say don't count. They may send you reeling with a sudden accusation. After thinking about the incident, you see how much they misunderstood. You may bring up the incident, ready to discuss it, but they say, "I don't remember saying that" or "That's not how I meant it" or they give themselves a quick excuse. They judge themselves by their intentions, not by how they affect others.

• **They have mastered the art of being emotionally fragile.** No matter how carefully you try to find a way to get them to listen, have empathy, or observe themselves, they will find a way to become upset. Then they try to make you feel guilty for upsetting them. In work settings, this individual is very difficult to give a performance evaluation to. Almost any effort to talk about doing better work or getting along better with others or being more direct in making requests triggers a defensive reaction. A good person may say, "Why are you picking on me? I'm not a bad person. Why don't you criticize Sheila? She's worse than I am." His reaction to your effort to make things better is to make you feel guilty for bringing up the subject of how he might improve.

- **Good people cannot distinguish between constructive and destructive criticism.** They react to unpleasant feedback as though it were destructive and had a harmful intent. They believe that if you really cared for them, you *would not confront them* about their upsetting actions. That is much different from a person with a survivor style who believes that if you care for her you *will confront her* about her upsetting actions. The consequence is that good people learn very little from experience. That is why a good person remains at the emotional level of a child throughout life.

- **They feel unloved and unappreciated.** Even though you give them lots of love and attention, they experience very little. They are like a person standing under a waterfall yelling, "I am thirsty!" Some typical statements: "After all I've done for them . . ." and "They'll feel sorry when I'm gone."

- **They are self-made martyrs.** First they blame you for their suffering, then they forgive you for all the hurt and pain you have caused them. As incredible as it may seem, the good child feels emotionally and morally superior to you.

- **Confronting them makes things worse.** If you get fed up and confront them about their victim style, they will have a victim reaction much worse than you've seen before. They cannot handle a confrontation about what they do because *the victim style is the best that they can manage.* As children, they have almost no capacity for self-observation or for conscious choices about thinking, feeling, or acting in different ways.

Thus the good-child syndrome is antithetical to the survivor style. Lacking emotional honesty and self-awareness, such a person suppresses paradoxical traits, avoids empathy, does not learn from experience, and has a desynergistic effect on others. He becomes stuck in destructive behavioral patterns and finds support from codependents around him, keeping them stuck in those patterns. Such a person can thwart your attempts at bringing about positive change because he perceives them as a personal attack. Although he may function fine from day to day, this is not the type of person you want to have in charge of something important.

Uncovering Hidden Barriers to Change: The Codependency Hang-Up

Often the biggest obstacle to change is change. Whenever a person repeats the same behavior pattern over and over, you can be certain that the person derives many emotional benefits from it. Codependency, for example, has been identified in recent years as an undesirable behavior pattern. Yet this is very difficult to change. Why? Because of the emotional payoffs a person gains from codependency. That and an inability to deal with the many fears stirred up by thoughts of changing.

Codependency is a term that came out of research attempting to understand why treatment efforts with individuals dependent on alcohol were seldom successful. The research discovered that alcohol dependency often occurs in a relationship in which a non-user gains many emotional benefits from rescuing and forgiving the user, much as how a good child feels she should act. The non-user, being indirectly dependent on the alcohol to provide her with the opportunity to do good, is thus codependent on it.

Perception Is Based on Contrast

Those who want to be seen as good need to create a contrast for themselves by portraying others as bad or defective in some way. The codependent husband or wife who constantly cares for, covers up for, and forgives the alcoholic spouse is often seen by close friends as a saint. This forgiving and loving person receives admiration and respect for bearing such a huge burden in life with unselfish dedication.

A less extreme but similar pattern is found in the way that some women get together and engage in ain't-men-awful complaining, as a female acquaintance once reported to me. It is a sort of bragging about how much they suffer because of the men in their lives. As with all repeated actions, there are benefits to the shared suffering. They experience close emotional intimacy with each other, closer often than with their partners. This activity helps explain why many men keep getting bad performance evaluations from their partners and cannot get an accurate job description. Their partners need fresh material for the next meeting.

According to conversations with Shale Paul, and as he wrote in his book *The Warrior Within: A Guide to Inner Power*, there are many hidden barriers working against those changing from being codependent or feeling like victims.

To change would mean to:

• Give up the negative frame of reference on which their identity is based.

- Lose a main source of esteem and appreciation from others.

- Appear to be tough, insensitive, and uncaring if they take a stand against the addicted person—that is, to have what children are told are signs of a bad person.

What may seem to be simple or easy changes for a person with survivor personality qualities feels emotionally insurmountable to the good person because this person has a constructed personality, not a discovered personality. Unfortunately for good people, the first attempts to help them break out of their dissatisfying patterns of codependency were seriously flawed.

The common practice of urging a person to declare, "I am a codependent" doesn't help her give up an undesirable behavior pattern and pressures her to accept a negative identity. This is abusive to someone whose self-esteem is already weak. It makes change more difficult when well-intentioned rescuers first urge the person to accept this negative identity, and then try to help her not be what she just became.

A better approach for you is to work toward replacing a dissatisfying, ineffective pattern of behavior from childhood or codependency with one that is more healthy, synergistic, and satisfying. This is easier said than done and will take time, thought, analysis, experimentation—and possibly some sessions with a counselor or coach—to identify your particular patterns and what replacement behaviors will work best for you.

Protecting Yourself

Of course there is nothing inherently bad about a person who tries to control others by getting upset or engaging others in a codependent relationship. The person often means well and has learned an effective way to cope with his circumstance. If you identify such people as being energy-draining sources in your own life, the question becomes, what can you do to be less vulnerable and less drained by them?

One possibility is to accept the situation as it is. Decide to pretend that things aren't as bad as they seem and just live with it.

Another option is to view the situation as a learning opportunity for yourself. What is to be learned? For one thing, you can stop allowing yourself to feel victimized by his victim style. Do you keep thinking to yourself that things would be so much better if only he would change? If so, you are reacting to his victim/blaming style with a victim/blaming reaction instead of a learning/coping reaction.

How can you react differently? Stop trying to get him to have empathy or observe himself. Stop spending hours trying to think up ways to get him to understand. Simply tell the person how you feel at each moment in response to what he has just said or done.

When you are accused of not caring or wanting to hurt him, try saying, "You're wrong," "It's too bad you let your mind think that way," or "You have it backward." Then be quiet. Do not explain your statement. Stop letting him avoid responsibility for the energy-draining effects of what he does and says.

Try shifting to a different level of communication. Realize that words will not work with such a person, any more than words can get a person addicted to drugs, alcohol, or gambling to change. Experiment with actions that will make him aware of the consequences of his behavior.

Be quick to praise improvement or any change for the better. Giving up an old way of doing things is easier when there are immediate benefits.

Breaking Free from Prohibitions: Difficult but Possible

If you find yourself relating to these good-child prohibitions, there is hope. It is important to recognize that the good-child codependent pattern was functional during childhood. It was a way of surviving. It was the best the child could do in a very difficult situation, and it worked. But as an adult it is restricting. The challenge for someone raised to be a good boy or girl is to develop new, additional ways of thinking, feeling, and acting. To do so requires courage because it means stepping outside the artificial shell of goodness into risky, even frightening territory.

Anyone trying to act like a good child is vulnerable to becoming overwhelmed when faced with challenges beyond the capacities of the act she was trained to perform. This is why good, well-behaved, white, middle-class young people, when faced with real-world problems, are often the most vulnerable to cults. After years of being praised for good conduct in school, it feels familiar to again sit passively in uncomfortable chairs without being allowed to go to the bathroom or get a drink of water until given permission. It feels familiar to passively sit and listen to an authoritative person tell them how to think, feel, and act to be a new kind of good [noun].

Having a survivor personality, in contrast, is not a way of being that can be learned from someone else telling you how to react. It is the emergence of your inborn abilities and level of awareness made possible by learning from your experiences and the experiences of others. It unfolds from within as emotionally constricting prohibitions are loosened and new opportunities are seen. The good-child syndrome is to act in a robotic way, while the survivor style is to take into account the situation at hand and act according to the effects of what one does.

THE chapters ahead show how real-life difficulties create better opportunities for developing new strengths than taking workshops or reading self-help books. The lessons are not easy, however, because to be more flexible often requires counterbalancing a good feeling or action with one that may have been labeled as bad. For people raised to be good, developing a survivor style usually requires learning to be more negative, selfish, angry, and self-appreciating.

The sequence of the following chapters is a progression. They show how disruptive change, distressing situations, and job loss often require thinking outside of your own comfort zone to become more skillful at handling difficult and unexpected situations.

Learning how to gain strength from these everyday difficulties, in turn, helps prepare you for handling crises, serious illness, disasters, and torturous experiences, should they occur. Your survivor strengths develop from learning and coping with daily, real life challenges given to you in the school of life.

NINE

Thriving

ADVERSITY comes in many forms. It may be a major life-disrupting change, many constant changes, or dozens of small pressures. Life's best survivors do more than cope with such adversities—they gain strength from them, they thrive.

Thriving During a Major Life-Disruptive Change

What would you do if your government seized your bank accounts, took possession of your business, physically removed you and your family from your home, and trucked you all to another part of the country—with orders to stay there?

This happened to many Japanese Americans in 1941. Shortly after the Japanese attacked Pearl Harbor and invaded the Philippines, the U.S. government quickly took into custody all Japanese Americans living on the Pacific Coast. Many were interned in guarded, barbed-wire compounds. Others were taken inland and, while allowed to rent private residences, were restricted to the local area.

The Naito family was taken to the outskirts of Salt Lake City, Utah. The father, Hide Naito, became despondent. He had been a good citizen. He had worked for years to build up his Norcrest China importing company. The family was very distressed. How could the U.S. government get away with taking everything they owned? It was un-American.

Sixteen-year-old Bill Naito looked at their situation. He knew they had to find a way to support themselves. He asked his family, "What can we do?" They needed a business that required very little capital; something the whole family could work at together.

Bill told me that he and his older brother, Sam, "came up with the idea of raising chickens and selling eggs. We obtained some chickens, carefully washed and packaged the eggs, and sold them to neighbors. We hatched more chickens, and produced more eggs. As the business grew, the whole family got involved, my mother, father, and sisters. We supported ourselves for four years selling eggs," Bill said, "and we had lots of chicken manure, so we traded it to a Japanese farmer for fresh vegetables." Smiling, Bill added, "Our business grew so big we built two large chicken coops—with concrete floors! The farming people around there had never heard of a chicken coop with concrete floors. They were amazed at us."

Some seventy years later, the Naito brother legacy is one for succeeding with major redevelopment projects that other developers wouldn't touch. As owners of more than a dozen businesses and many commercial buildings, they have won many awards for reshaping the downtown area of Portland, Oregon, with their daring ventures.

Bill Naito said, "Dreams come from difficulties. The question 'What can we do?' leads to imagination, to exploring possible solutions. I like it when someone says that what we have in mind is impossible."

Gaining Strength from Adversity

In comments about psychologically healthy people, Abraham Maslow referred to the *continental divide principle*. He said, "I use this principle to describe the fact that stress will either break people altogether if they are in the beginning too weak to stand distress, or else, if they are already strong enough to take the stress in the first place, that same stress, if they come through it, will strengthen them, temper them, and make them stronger."

How do some people thrive, gain strength while others in the same circumstances get weaker? What makes the difference?

People who thrive follow a similar pattern of actions and reactions after being knocked off track by disruptive change. They:

- Regain emotional balance.

- Cope during the transition.

- Adapt to the new reality.

- Recover to a stable condition.

- Thrive by learning to be better and stronger than before.

The following diagram shows the thriving sequence and different ways people react to disruptive life changes:

Some attack those they blame for upsetting their lives. Some feel overwhelmed and they go numb. Those who become victims

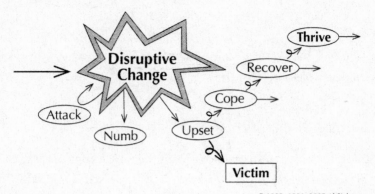

feel ruined for life. Others eventually cope with the disaster but never fully recover and become stuck at some level. People who thrive move through these stages and expect things to turn out well. While at first they may get upset about the disruptive change, their positive attitude will start to spiral them upward toward a beneficial outcome. With an optimistic spirit, thrivers begin to ask all sorts of questions: What is happening? What is the new reality? What can I do? Why is it good that this happened? Often they notice something amusing in the midst of the drama. They use empathy and creative thinking to imagine an outcome they believe could work. They act with self-confidence when they experiment with learning a better way to do something and remain flexible about unexpected developments.

The Sequence: Handle Feelings First

To regain emotional balance from such major disruptive life change as job loss or divorce, the important first steps are to express your feelings and join together with others for mutual support. Psychologist James Pennebaker and his associates used an emotions-writing technique with a group of skilled workers who had lost their jobs because of downsizing in a major corporation and had not been successful in finding new employment.

Eight months after writing about their emotions for twenty minutes a day for five days, 68 percent of the participants had full-time or satisfactory part-time employment; 48 percent of a matched group that wrote about their time-management plans had employment; only 27 percent of a nonparticipating group had found work.

Pennebaker reports in unpublished research and in his book *Opening Up* that during their interviews, all the people in the group who wrote about their feelings said they wished they had written about their feelings sooner. They had not done well in job interviews, they admitted, because they had not handled their feelings effectively.

Why a Support Group Is Helpful

During a disruptive life change, it is extremely helpful to spend time with others who will listen while you talk. A support group can help you get through the crazy period when your mind is obsessed with negative thoughts and feelings about ex-bosses or the soon-to-be ex-spouse.

When managers reduce the size of their workforce, there is no way to do it right. Workers have an endless litany of complaints about how the executives and managers are doing it wrong and how their incompetence created the situation in the first place.

The same is true during a divorce. Your mind can repeat over and over what the other person is doing wrong and what she should be doing differently. Past experiences come welling up and get added to long internal conversations, rehashing all the things the other person should know about herself while feeling frustrated because she doesn't want to hear it.

A support group can help you get through all this and refocus your energy in a positive direction.

The Cumulative Effects: Some Get Bitter, Some Get Better

People stuck in the victim pattern, as illustrated below, accumulate negative experiences and their capacity to handle strain diminishes.

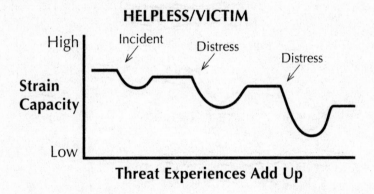

HELPLESS/VICTIM

Threat Experiences Add Up

People who thrive become stronger and more capable. Their self-confidence increases as each disruptive experience is surmounted, as shown on the next page.

The effect is similar to what the Outward Bound programs purposefully arrange for their participants. Henry W. Taft, former Outward Bound president, said in the preface to Robert Godfrey's *Outward Bound: Schools of the Possible* that the program experiences "teach you to survive in the wilderness of life." He goes on to say they give a person the feeling, "If I can do this, I can do anything."

LEARNING/THRIVING

Threat Experiences Diminish

Each experience involving disruptive changes can teach you how to go through the thriving sequence in days or hours rather than months. Each challenge is quickly processed as just another incident (rather than a distress) and converted into a new adventure. You can feel the distress, take steps to cope with the transition, ask for help from family and friends, locate useful resources, develop Plan A and Plan B, and move forward with enthusiasm about having a new life direction. Movement, rather than inertia, is what makes the difference.

A New Direction

I conducted a workshop at a large chemical fertilizer plant to help employees cope with a 70 percent reduction in the workforce. Many of them felt shocked, bewildered, and despondent about the future. Four months later, after the layoffs had been completed, I returned to the plant to conduct a team-building workshop with the managers, employees, and supervisors who had been retained. As I walked across the parking lot with one of the few remaining supervisors, I asked him, "How does it feel to be one of the survivors?"

He looked around as though to make sure we wouldn't be overheard and said, "Frankly, Al, I'm kind of disappointed."

"You are?"

"When corporate headquarters announced the layoffs, I assumed I'd get the ax. I always wanted to get a college education, so I wrote away for catalogs. I talked to several advisers, picked my courses, and had my application forms all filled out. I was ready to send in my check the day my layoff letter arrived." He smiled and said, "I'm glad to have a job, but disappointed about having to postpone college."

I could understand why the plant managers had decided to keep him and let most of the others go. Whatever life threw at him, he was ready with a positive new plan.

Who Is Responsible?

How well or how poorly we react to disruptive change boils down to an important difference in people. That difference is how we answer the question, Who is basically responsible for the way my life goes?

Psychologist Julian Rotter found that some people believe that the primary point of control in their lives is inside themselves. He described them as people with an "internal locus of control." Rotter refers to those who believe that the primary point of control in their lives is outside themselves, as having an "external locus of control." (Read more about this in Chapter 10.)

People who thrive in difficult situations reflect internal attitudes and beliefs. People who go numb, feel victimized, or lash out angrily reflect external beliefs.

A Demonstration Test

The statements in the following chart, adapted from the sample test developed by Rotter, demonstrate some differences between internal and external feelings of control. For each of the pairs of statements, check the one that most closely reflects your belief.

Which statement do you agree with the most, the one on the left or the right?

____Promotions usually come from being liked by the right people.	____Most promotions are earned through hard work and persistence.
____Nowadays, luck determines income more than ability.	____In our society, a person's income is determined mostly by ability.
____I have little control over events that affect my life.	____The things that happen to me are about what I deserve.
____Luck determines success or failure in life.	____Almost anyone can be successful with good planning and hard work.
____I would be happier if the world didn't have so many problems.	____A person can be happy even when there are many problems.

SCORING: The statements on the left side reflect external locus of control beliefs. The statements on the right side reflect internal locus of control beliefs.

A fascinating finding in this research is that both sets of beliefs are self-validating. People who believe their fate is under the control of outside forces act in a way that confirms that belief. People who know they can do things to make life better act in a way that confirms their belief.

Thriving During Constant Change

The more internally directed you are, the better you will be at thriving in conditions of many smaller, constant changes. These frequent smaller changes can sneak up on you and accumulate, one by one, without being fully noticed. Because you are aware of these subtle occurrences—even subconsciously—you adjust to this, adapt to that, and keep on going.

In today's world, where change has become constant, new skills are needed. In the past we could expect that a change was a one-time event to be gotten through until things settled down again. In the past, we could settle into a job and expect to keep it until retirement. People coming into the workforce today have to be prepared for four, five, or six careers.

In the past, a company might change hands once in a worker's lifetime. A relative getting divorced was a rare occurrence. You might never receive a notice from your bank informing you that it has a new name because it was purchased by a larger company. Now such changes are frequent.

All these changes come with an emotional price. Your energy is stretched thin. You feel irritated when your favorite store moves to a different location or goes out of business. You may feel a bit lost, as if the world you are living in wasn't one you know.

To handle constant change effectively requires that you first be conscious of the changes. Take some time to look at the following list of ways of experiencing life that applies to actions, thoughts, and behaviors of the past and how these are different from the now. Add more differences taken from your own experience. It would be very helpful to get together with others to talk about these changes.

PAST	NOW
future certain	future uncertain
plan long term	plan temporary
resist change	manage change
reliance on leaders	reliance on self
trained to fit into stable organization	coached to change with organizational change
trained for existing job	learn to create job
know the answers	know the questions
seek safety, avoid risk	manage risk
eliminate stress	handle stress
loyalty to organization	loyalty to profession
job focus on the product	job focus on service
avoid mistakes, errors	learn from errors
trained to be good	learn effective habits
disagreement suppressed	disagreement encouraged
safe conditions at work, home	unsafe at work, home

two-parent families	single-parent families
children watched by older adults	children watch television
rigid male and female roles	male and female roles unclear
long-term goals	instant gratification
invent games to play	buy games to play
common moral values	moral values unclear
infrequent bad news	frequent bad news
earth absorbed human activities	earth overwhelmed by human activities
die earlier	live longer
_____	_____
_____	_____

Change requires learning throughout your life. Change also means letting go of the past. And transitioning from the past is helped by spending some time remembering and talking about the good old days that will never return.

In a way, it is like the mourning process: you remember, then move on. To facilitate the emotional side of the changes, get together with a few people and interview each other about your best memories. What are you proud of? What do you feel sad about losing? What do you feel glad to get away from?

Then ask, What is better now than before? What is good about all the changes taking place?

Thriving During a Major Ongoing Challenge

To thrive means to find value and opportunity in events outside your control. Jim Dyer had worked as a state employee for more than twenty years when a new director was appointed to run his agency. At a meeting with agency managers, the director announced a reorganization plan that would ruin years of good work done by field office managers. Jim told me, "I spoke up and asked a question about implementing the plan. The director glared at me. He got very angry. He said, 'Jim, your problem is you aren't a team player.' "

Three weeks later, the administrator reassigned Jim to a different position. A month after that, he was transferred to a different department. A few months later, he was reassigned to another office. A year after that, he was transferred to a new position, then to another agency section, and so on.

What was Jim's reaction to each transfer? "I like people," he says. "I like doing things for people. Each morning I'd say to myself, 'This is a fresh chance to do something for people.' Plus I had interests outside my job. I did not depend on my work for feelings of importance to others."

Jim learned each new position quickly and made himself useful. He enjoyed each new challenge and liked having a chance to learn about different offices and units. He says that after six years of being bounced from position to position, "a deputy director confided to me that the director of the agency had tried to get section heads to reduce me in grade or force me to quit, but they had not complied because they could never find grounds. I was always too capable and useful."

In fact, Jim's status began to increase. Because of the knowledge he had gained about the inner workings of many state agencies, he became a special troubleshooter handling citizen's complaints. Then, two years before he retired, he got an unexpected reward. He says, "When the job classifiers looked at what I was doing, they jumped me three pay grades, from a twenty-four to a twenty-seven! And I didn't even give them all the documentation they usually need. I retired at a much higher grade than I expected!"

Overcoming the Illusion of Stress

Jim Dyer's ability to effectively handle a situation at work that would have stressed out most people is typical of life's best survivors. Instead of reacting like a victim and eventually filing a stress disability claim, he thrived.

The term *stress*, as it is commonly used, is a misnomer, promulgated in part because of a mistake made by Hans Selye, the physician who did the pioneering research on what he termed "biological stress."

Selye, a medical doctor with a PhD in organic chemistry, conducted research to learn why the body's glands and organs react in a similar way to many different diseases, illnesses, and toxins (poisons). He wanted to understand the physiology of being sick. His research led him to discover what he called the general adaptation syndrome (GAS). The GAS showed how illness and death can occur when constant alarm reactions (sometimes called the fight-or-flight response) exhaust the body's response capacities. Selye found that high blood pressure, heart attacks, ulcers, decreased immune system resistance, and physiological exhaustion are not the result of specific diseases. They are "diseases of adaptation." That is, they occur when the body's ability to respond to constant demands becomes exhausted.

However, Selye confessed in his memoirs, *The Stress of My Life: A Scientist's Memoirs*, that he had used the wrong term to describe how the body's adaptive resources become exhausted. He wrote:

> In seeking a name for my theory, I borrowed [a] term from physics, where "stress" refers to the interaction between a force and the resistance to it. I merely added an adjective to emphasize that I was using the term in a special sense, and baptized my [conceptual] child "biological stress." But frankly, when I made this choice I did not . . . know the difference between "stress" and "strain." In physics, "stress" refers to an agent that acts upon a resistant body attempting to deform it, whereas "strain" indicates the changes that are induced in the affected object. Consequently I should have called my findings the "strain syndrome. . . ." I did not distinguish between the causative agent and its effect upon the body.

In other words, the challenge for each of us is strain, not stress. The world is not filled with stressors darting around like invisible piranha eating away at you. There is no stress in any situation until you feel strain.

Surveys identifying job stresses and workshops on job stress reduction are often more harmful than helpful in that they mislead people and have spawned an explosion in stress disability claims. For example, whether a person experiences stress at work depends on the person's perception of what is going on and the person's coping skills. It is not the circumstance; it is your reaction to it that counts.

What is stressful for one person is not stressful for another.

This means that job stress cannot be objectively defined. The distress a person may feel is not a result of what actually exists objectively in the job. It is a result of how the person perceives what is happening.

For example, if a weightlifter loses control of a hundred-pound barbell held overhead and drops it toward another athlete, will it be stressful for this person to try to catch the barbell? Yes, if she is a slender teenage girl, even if she is a medal-winning gymnast. It is very likely she would be hurt trying to catch the barbell. But if the other athlete is a professional football lineman, he might catch the barbell in one hand and hand it back saying, "Did you drop this?" For him, a hundred-pound barbell is not enough weight to give him a good workout.

The point is that a hundred-pound barbell is just a hundred-pound barbell. It is not a harmful stressor until a person trying to lift it feels strained beyond her or his strength level.

If you had to handle three hundred telephone calls a day from people wanting some sort of action from your company, would that be stressful? For most of us it would. But for the customer service representatives at an insurance company who handle on average more than four hundred calls a day, three hundred would be an easy day.

Many people have also missed the point that a strain can be beneficial. Selye coined the term *eustress* to emphasize that some strain is necessary for good health. A moderate level is most desirable. Athletes build up their physical strength through frequent workouts. Professional schools build competence by pushing people to their limits and slightly beyond. Distressing experiences can motivate people to learn new coping skills.

For these reasons, then, books, articles, and workshops on job stress reduction are often more harmful than helpful because they create the illusion that something called stress is out there, constantly assaulting and harming each of us. In truth, what most people call stress is really an internal feeling of strain that they don't like.

Why Stress Is an Important Concern

No matter what term is used, if you want a long and healthy life, it is important to understand the many ways that stress and strain affect the human body. Humans with bodies like ours first appeared on the planet about a hundred thousand years ago. For most of that time, the average lifespan was about thirty-five years. In the last hundred years or so—as humans identified and controlled contagious diseases and infections through sanitary practices, personal hygiene, vaccinations, and antibiotics—the average life expectancy worldwide climbed to fifty and then to sixty years. Then, with increased longevity, poor lifestyle choices were discovered to be a significant cause of death. People were shortening their lives through smoking, drinking, unhealthy eating, reckless living, and lack of exercise. New knowledge about the importance of physical fitness, nutrition, and safe living led to an increased average life expectancy to nearly seventy years.

Today, heart attacks, cancer, and strokes are listed as the main causes of death. Even people with good physical and nutritional habits were dying from what Selye identified decades previously as diseases of adaptation.

But is stress the problem? No. The problem is that some people react to circumstances and events in their lives in ways that lead to illness and early death. The real killer is too much constant strain, and the victims are often its accomplices.

Many people are self-frazzling. They bring on diseases of ad-

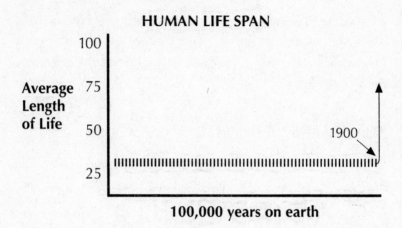

aptation through poor self-management. Evidence that humans generally do not know how to handle emotional strain very well is found in the widespread use of tranquilizers, drugs, and alcohol. According to the National Institute on Drug Abuse, Americans obtain millions of prescriptions for Valium, Xanax, Prozac, and other anxiety- and depression-reducing medications every year. Millions of additional people use alcohol, drugs, and other substances to reduce tension and relax.

Illness-Susceptible Versus Illness-Resistant Behaviors

A great deal of research has been conducted to determine the possible relationships between illness and human behavior. This research indicates that individuals more likely to develop illnesses related to the strain syndrome:

- Experience distress in routine activities.

- Feel vulnerable, helpless, and without choices.

- Have limited internal and external resources on which to draw.

- Are not sure what they feel and can't express feelings easily.

- Blame others for their unpleasant feelings ("You upset me").

- Feel socially isolated, not accepted.

- Have little capacity for self-change.

- Accumulate negative experiences.

In contrast, those who are less likely to develop illnesses related to the strain syndrome:

- Seldom experience distress in routine activities.

- Feel capable of taking effective action about upsetting events.

- Draw action choices from a wide range of inner and external resources.

- Experience family and friends as caring and supportive.

- Know how they feel and can express feelings.

- Separate their reactions from the cause ("I feel upset about what you did").

- Manage self-change well.

- Convert negative experiences into beneficial learning.

- Actively pursue positive, enjoyable experiences.

There is a pattern here that is similar to how our cells react to a foreign substance. Allergic reactions occur when our cells mistakenly interpret food or benign substances as toxic. When a person has an allergic reaction to wheat or dairy products, for example, the cells react as though the substance were a poison. Selye explained that if a cell interprets a substance as toxic, it has a *catatoxic* reaction—that is, its reaction is to destroy the toxin. If the cell interprets the substance as not harmful, it has a *syntoxic* reaction. It puts up with it.

Some people appear to have allergic minds. They feel alarmed and distressed about many ordinary events. Conversely, some people develop strong mental and emotional immunities to circumstances and events that upset others. They convert what others experience as toxic into something nutritious.

The situation is similar to how people react to bee stings. A few people are so allergic that they are at risk of dying if stung by one or two bees. Most people have a normal catatoxic reaction to a bee sting. The spot swells up as the body's defenses isolate the bee venom and work to destroy it. Beekeepers, however, have a syntoxic reaction to bee stings. They have such an immunity to the toxin that they have little reaction to many stings. Emotional immunity is like that. It is acquired by learning from experience.

Overcoming Inner Restrictions

People raised to be good children often have difficulty dealing with life's various strains because they were raised to not complain or be unhappy and to not be selfish. Yet to avoid developing diseases of adaptation one must be able to express unhappiness and act in ways that may seem selfish.

To feel unhappy and negative for a few hours is like letting yourself fall down when you've lost your balance. You do it and then get up. A person who sometimes expresses negative thinking is not the same as a person who is negative all the time.

One day I telephoned a friend, Joanne, who is a psychiatric nurse. We hadn't talked in over a year. When she heard it was me on the phone, she said, "Oh, Al! You would call today of all days! I feel miserable! My mother is visiting and yesterday she had several of her friends over for breakfast. They went into the den and got so busy talking they forgot about the skillet with sausage on the stove. It caught fire and set fire to my kitchen cabinets. Now my kitchen will have to be rebuilt. . . .

"I got a call from my daughter's school. They're having a problem with her so I have to go see the school counselor. I feel very upset about that. . . .

"Yesterday I said something very stupid during a meeting. I feel really embarrassed. . . .

"This morning I decided to paint an old bookcase. I spilled the paint and have paint splattered on me. . . ."

She paused for a moment and then said, "You know, Al, it's too bad that more people don't know how to enjoy feeling depressed."

I laughed. Here is the best psychiatric nurse I know, one of the most durable, hardy, synergistic people I've ever met, having a good time feeling miserable.

She went on to say, "I'm giving myself until four p.m. to enjoy this. Then I have to clean up and go to a dinner meeting."

Joanne knows that letting yourself feel really negative about things once in a while does not make you a negative person. Just the opposite. It is a sign of excellent mental health. People who try to program themselves to have only positive feelings are fragile. They need a protective environment because they don't handle pressure or conflict well.

Thriving Under Life's Strains

One way guaranteed to increase your distressing experiences is to not want to be where you are. Your emotional distress decreases by deciding, like a flower seed, to bloom where you are planted.

If you want to handle your life situation better, follow this simple two-part method for decreasing strain, avoiding feeling helpless and hopeless, and maintaining and growing vitality:

1. A. Make a list of everything you find irritating and upsetting. Ask, What upsets me? Makes me feel unhappy? Feels stressful? Take your time. Play it up.

   B. Wait a while and then go through the list of negative experiences, item by item, asking questions such as:

   - What if I ignored this? What if I avoided contact?

   - Could I do something about this? What could I do to change what bothers me?

   - Can I make it go away? Get it out of my life?

   - If I can't avoid it, change it, or make it go away, what if I changed my reaction to it? What if I decided to stop letting it bother me?

   - What can I learn from this? Why is it *good* that this happens?

   C. Select one or two items on the list and develop a plan of action for making some changes.

2. A. Make a list of what revitalizes you. List what you find invigorating and fun. Ask yourself these questions:

    • What do I have fun doing? Get enthusiastic about?

    • What would I like to do that I keep putting off?

    • With whom do I enjoy sharing good experiences?

    • Am I ignoring or taking for granted some positive aspects of my life?

    B. Ask questions about how to repeat, increase, or have new positive experiences.

    C. Develop a plan of action for increasing positive, revitalizing experiences.

This personalized plan is an effective way to decrease distressing experiences and increase revitalizing ones. The result is that you avoid feeling helpless and hopeless; you continuously learn new ways of making your life better.

Keep in mind that time plays a part in this. Certain pressures can be changed today, others will take a year or so, and still others may take longer. Some pleasant activities may take a while to bring about. In the long run, however, this is a very practical way to lessen overload sensations and replace them with positive anticipations about your future.

If you feel constant stress and are not taking action to improve your situation, ask yourself, "What prevents me from handling my situation better and finding ways to enjoy my life and work? What benefits do I derive from having things as they are? What are some payoffs I don't want to give up?" The benefits of inaction are many. The list includes not needing much energy (to sustain things as they are), not accepting responsibility for bad outcomes (for changes not made), and receiving praise for being so steadfast (your inaction). It may be that you derive so many indirect benefits from being harried and overworked, you can't imagine life without them.

IN *The Road Less Traveled*, M. Scott Peck says, "Wise people learn not to dread but actually to welcome problems." The school of life arranges for great learning opportunities for people who react to difficulties by learning new skills. The chapters ahead show how to learn and even thrive in situations that other people react to by feeling frustrated or victimized.

TEN

The Roots of Resiliency
Your Inner "Selfs"

A GROUP of about 180 state managers sat talking with subdued voices. Severe strain showed on many faces. They had just learned that in the months ahead more than four thousand state employees would be laid off and most departments would be reorganized. Many of the managers would be demoted to their last clerical position or laid off. Never before, in their many decades of public service, had they ever faced such devastating changes.

Losing your job through no fault of your own can be extremely distressing. When an organization lays people off, it does not matter that you have worked hard and gotten excellent performance evaluations. Your job is eliminated; you are out of work.

People react to job loss in different ways. A few are resilient and cope well. They rebound quickly, orient to the new situation, and start dealing with it. For some, the situation is so devastating they go into emotional shock. Others feel like victims, blaming management, politicians, foreign competition—anyone—for what has happened.

With thousands of people being laid off, it turns out that white males in midlevel management positions are the most emotionally devastated by job loss due to budget cuts, downsizing, and reorganization. Many of them feel deeply distressed despite assistance with résumé writing, outplacement services, and job interview coaching.

The unemployment crisis has uncovered a hidden weakness in many male managers. Their sense of identity and feelings of worth have been based not on an inner sense of who and what they are, but on external proofs of masculinity. The validation of being a man was derived from job title, office location, budget amount, number of people managed, and income level.

Men who find themselves taking college classes to prepare for new careers often report feeling diminished. Men who register for unemployment benefits while their wives bring home a paycheck often feel depressed. Their job loss is more than an unemployment crisis; it is also an identity crisis.

Guidelines for overcoming the sense of inner weakness that keeps a person from coping well will be covered later in this chapter. First, however, it is important to examine and understand the roots of human resiliency. Crises that require you to manage your own survival force you to develop your inner resources. While there are many services and external resources available to you during such rough developments as job loss, divorce, bankruptcy, or disabling injury, you will not be able to utilize those resources effectively unless you also draw upon your inner resources.

Thriving in Adversity:
Developing Stronger Inner "Selfs"

Our bodies have three major nervous systems: the autonomic, somatic, and central. The autonomic nervous system governs the state of our feelings. The somatic controls our physical actions. The central nervous system contains the cerebral cortex that makes possible our verbal, conceptual thinking and nonverbal, visual thinking.

As we grow up we develop a sense of ourselves linked to the three major nervous systems. We develop feelings about ourselves, we anticipate our ability to take effective actions, and we develop thoughts about ourselves. These internal experiences of one's self are referred to as self-esteem, self-confidence, and self-concept. When they are strong, positive, and healthy, you can cope well with life adversities. If your inner resources are not strong, you tend to suffer more and cope less well. Understanding how these systems function and how they affect you is crucial to developing your inner resources.

- **Self-esteem** is your emotional opinion of yourself. It is how you feel about yourself as a person. A demotion, job loss, or divorce may uncover how your feelings of self-esteem were derived from your job title, paycheck, or social role. But these external points of reference are not the real source of anyone's self-esteem. People with weak self-esteem often exaggerate or cling to external proofs of their importance to compensate for a lack of self-esteem. The emotional benefit you can gain from a change in your status is to realize that positive regard for yourself is essential for coping with losing external proofs of how special you are.

People with strong self-esteem feel less vulnerable to the negative opinions of others. Their self-esteem acts like a thick energy blanket around them. It enables them to shrug off hurtful criticisms and lets them accept compliments.

People with strong self-esteem neither play up nor play down their accomplishments. There is a kind of solidity or stability to them, as if their core were not affected by the opinions of others. You may feel this way sometimes, and yet vulnerable at other times. The good news is that strong self-esteem can be developed during challenging times. The more frequently you appreciate yourself, despite what goes on around you, the more you will feel good about your deepest self.

- **Self-confidence** refers to how well you expect to do in a new activity. It is an action predictor. Generally this confidence is based on your reliable abilities and strengths. People lacking self-confidence feel they cannot rely on themselves, so they avoid risky efforts. These people suffer a great deal of anxiety when unwillingly thrown into a situation that requires them to perform unfamiliar work or navigate in unknown territory.

  People with strong self-confidence know they can count on themselves even more than they can count on anyone else. People who exhibit impressive self-reliance have strong self-confidence. Such people expect to handle adversities and succeed in new activities.

- **Self-concept** refers to your idea about who and what you are. Some of your self-concept may have been based on your occupation or employment by an organization. Many out-of-work auto and construction workers are having a difficult time retraining for new careers because their identities have been based on their work.

Some people go to great lengths to prop up their self-concept. The need for a positive self-concept is so strong that some people will lie about what they have accomplished and how much they earn. Others deny immoral or unethical actions when confronted because they cannot handle the truth that they acted as they did. Some try to compensate for a weak self-concept with impressive clothing, titles, high income, important friends, the right address, outstanding children, and other external proofs of being successful. That is why they are so devastated when they lose those external proofs.

Why Strong Inner Selfs Are Essential

People coping with job loss need the inner strength that comes from healthy, positive inner selfs. Healthy self-esteem, strong self-confidence, and a positive self-concept give one the ability to shrug off almost being hired and to go into the next interview feeling positive. A person looking for a good position needs to demonstrate to prospective employers how well he or she can hold up under pressure, quickly grasp and empathize with the employer's needs, and accurately and confidently state his or her qualifications for the job.

People going through a breakup in their relationship survive the emotional blow better when their inner selfs are strong. People who don't cope well may have been relying on their spouses to compensate for deficits in their self-esteem or self-concept, which may have contributed to the breakup in the first place.

Women and men who have been abused often find emotional recovery very difficult, but the process is made easier in a group with other survivors (not victims), where each person is encouraged to develop strong conscious feelings of positive self-regard, rebuild self-concept, and develop self-confidence. People with physical differences, those who find themselves in a minority, or those who are the target of hurtful rumors also need a strong inner buffer between the self they know and the hostile talk.

Almost daily we witness the lack of strong selfs in some young celebrities, especially those who grow up in the spotlight and are constantly fighting against tabloid rumors. Looking for approval, they tend to bare their souls to the media, which sometimes makes things worse. The celebrities whose lives you rarely hear about have developed a strong sense of self and have no need to shout to the world that the tabloid reports are wrong.

Anyone whose work is in the public eye needs a strong inner identity because much of the public has a preconceived notion of what they should do. When public officials, editors, and school superintendents, for example, act in ways outside of a widely held stereotype, they routinely receive letters and phone calls telling them what they're doing wrong.

Your Inner Selfs Determine
How Well Your Life Progresses

Strong self-esteem, solid self-confidence, and a positive self-concept provide the inner foundation for:

- Recovering from major setbacks such as unemployment, divorce, disfigurement, or loss of a loved one.

- Setting challenging goals, imagining yourself as successful, and handling success when it occurs.

- Accepting praise, recognition, and friendship as legitimate.

- Learning from mistakes and failures.

- Not being pressured into undesirable actions or situations out of fear of being disliked.

- Resisting being manipulated by insincere flattery.

- Rejecting undeserved criticism as something to ignore.

- Admitting mistakes and apologizing to others for them.

- Handling new, unexpected developments, knowing you can count on yourself.

- Building your identity on being a unique, special human being.

A Self-Strength Assessment

A person may be strong in one self-dimension and weak in another. To determine how strong your different aspects of self are, ask yourself the following questions:

- Am I reluctant to engage in self-praise? Do I avoid thoughts and feelings of self-appreciation? What do I fear might happen if I think nice things about myself?

- How do I react when someone compliments me? Do I accept it graciously or quickly dismiss it?

- Do I like how I dress? What is the condition of my car? My bedroom? Does the place where I live and sleep show that I regard myself as a special person?

- When faced with a difficult challenge, do I know I can count on myself to handle it well? Am I pleased to have me on my side?

- What kind of self-talk do I engage in? Do I tear myself down? Scold myself? Call myself names? Try to beat people to the punch and criticize myself first? Do I encourage myself? Give myself pep talks?

- How do I describe myself? What is my identity? Have I developed professionalism in the work I do?

Your ability to handle adversities, either minor or major, is determined by these three inner selfs. If they are weak, they can handicap your efforts. If strong, they can be an invaluable resource. The stronger all of them are, the more you have a personal advantage in difficult situations.

How to Build a Strong Team of Selfs

DEVELOPING STRONG SELF-ESTEEM

One way to start to develop a stronger self-esteem is to separate your opinion of yourself from negative or critical opinions others might have about you. This may sound difficult if you haven't done it before, but it is an emotional distinction that can be practiced and developed.

Take time to make a list of all the ways you value yourself and feel good about yourself. Become aware of your self-talk. You may need to take a strong grip on your inner dialogue and to repeat things like, "Despite what has happened, I like myself." Become a staunch supporter of your inner sense of your worth and value. Honor yourself, even if others don't. Make a list of what you like and appreciate about yourself.

MAKE A LIST

I like and appreciate that I am _____.

This self-appreciating activity buffers you against insensitive comments from others. If you have been laid off, acquaintances and neighbors may want to know why. Even though you may be wondering the same thing, you need to have a comeback ready, almost like having a good return in a tennis match, so that you won't be thrown off balance by a sudden question.

If someone says the downsizing is to get rid of some of the dead wood, be ready to set him straight. If you have assessed what you like about yourself ahead of time and know, for example, that you are proficient at your job, you will be well equipped to say something like, "The layoffs are being handled on the basis of least seniority—not competence." If you have been through a divorce, have some sort of short statement ready for the times when someone asks, "What happened?" By listing your self-appreciated traits you can develop a response that doesn't make you look weak.

Every time you choose to have high self-esteem in the face of others' negativity, you become strengthened and inwardly freed from the ups and downs of circumstance. This kind of self-esteem makes up the difference between the feedback you receive from others and what you need psychologically to sustain yourself.

BUILDING SELF-CONFIDENCE

Memories of past accomplishments and awareness of praiseworthy abilities are not usually uppermost in the mind of a person going through an unwanted, disruptive change—but they need to be! To give yourself proper perspective, make a list of all the things you've done well.

MAKE A LIST

My reliable strengths and abilities are that I _____.

This activity will provide you with a list of skills you know you can perform well.

After you have created the list of your reliable strengths, practice talking about your strengths to another person. Choose a good friend to help you with this exercise. Not only will this exercise strengthen your self-confidence but it will help you overcome the false modesty that you may have adopted because you were trained not to be a braggart.

The list of all the things you've done well in the past is an excellent way to give you the evidence of your worth that will allow you to feel confident.

Part of coping well is to remind yourself of past times when you have survived and surmounted bad situations. Employees who have been through layoffs with previous employers know that they will handle this one as well. Most people with disabilities know that the road to a better future will be rough but that it can be managed.

ENHANCING YOUR SELF-CONCEPT

Many times when we try to think of who we are we come up with nouns for roles such as "I am a manager" or "I am Sally's husband." But what happens if the external frame of reference for the role disappears? Where is your identity now?

To help get away from roles as a source of identity, take a moment to check out whom you would be if the external basis for your identity disappeared. For example, like the television show *Survivor*, imagine being shipwrecked on an island with several other people, but this time, survival of everyone is top priority. What role would you play in the new community? Would you still be funny and compassionate? Brave about taking risks? Would you be a natural leader, or are you best at supporting someone who takes charge? Taking away the scenery from your current life can sometimes help you identify the real you and thus put a more concrete self-concept in place.

What if you lived in another time in history, as in the Wild West or in an ancient civilization? What would you be like? You would still be you—the real you—wearing a toga perhaps and doing different things, but your personal attributes would be the same. These qualities—perseverance, quickness, gentleness, or whatever you see—are the genuine components of your self-concept. If you can image that you would still be you in another century, another place, or on a reality TV show, you can rest assured that you will still be you in another job or in another relationship.

Completing the statement "I am . . ." ten or more times will bring out your thoughts about yourself. These thoughts work like instructions that affect your beliefs about yourself and therefore about your capabilities. Make a list about your self-concept.

MAKE A LIST

I am _____.

It could be helpful to talk about this list with a good friend or with a support group. It is not easy to learn how to base your identity on your personal qualities, abilities, and values instead of your roles, but it is worth the effort. The less your identity depends on a job title, social role, or marital status, the more inner strength you have for coping with major life transitions when these external props are yanked out from under you. When your three main dimensions of self are strong, you believe in yourself, you like yourself, and you can cope well.

What to Expect

Strengthening and developing your inner dimensions of self can change your relationships. Sometimes, however, the change may not be easy for others to handle. Some married soldiers returning from war zones find that their wives have developed strong self-confidence as a result of being forced to make their own decisions, arrange for repairs, take care of finances, and deal with home emergencies. People who develop strong self-confidence seldom regress. Many wives are not willing to resume a dependent relationship, and some marriages do not survive.

On the other hand, some people in your life may be greatly relieved when you gain inner strength. Trying to live and work with a person with weak selfs is usually an energy drain on everyone. Instead of reacting negatively to the stronger you, some of the important people in your life may say to you, "It's about time!" Everyone is happier.

A Paradoxical Balance

Even though life can seem unfair when people in powerful positions break the rules, keep in mind that there are no rules limiting what you can do to survive, cope, and thrive. Life's best survivors draw power from the laws and forces of nature and their paradoxical inner strengths.

My research has taught me that the most resilient people in rough situations are those with a:

- Balance between self-esteem and self-criticism.

- Blend of self-confidence and self-doubt.

- Positive self-concept open to accept the existence of flaws and weaknesses.

A person who is self-critical without self-appreciation seldom accomplishes much. Furthermore, the person who is constantly self-appreciating without self-criticism seldom admits to mistakes, weaknesses, and errors. This could lead to missing important chances for learning. In other words, the selfs in resilient, thriving people are paradoxical.

Review and Preview

Take some time now to look back through the guidelines and recommended steps for developing strong inner selfs. Keep in mind that none of this is a quick fix. Emotional work is not easy. As a process, it can be hard work and you may have relapses. The payoff is worthwhile, however. Strong inner selfs help you survive and surmount difficulties of all kinds. In the following chapters you will see how being forced to deal with illness, crisis, disaster, or even cruelty can result in discovering personal strengths you would never have believed possible.

ELEVEN

Self-Managed Healing

The Dreaded Words

Joyce noticed a boil on the inside of her left arm as she got ready for bed, but she felt too tired to be concerned. She had just been through an emotionally exhausting divorce and custody fight for her two children. She was working long hours at the bank branch she managed. At home, she often stayed up late doing household chores after her children went to bed. She wasn't sleeping well at night because of a persistent cough that disturbed her. "I was thirty and had always been healthy," she says, "I thought I just needed to take more vitamins."

In the morning she found two more boils on her arm. By noon more had spread up her arm and neck, so she went to an emergency medical clinic. From the clinic she was sent to a hospital for more testing.

The next day she returned to the hospital to learn the results.

When she saw the grim look on the doctor's face, her heart pounded so hard she was sure he could hear it. "I'm sorry to have to tell you this," he said, "but you have leukemia, a cancer of the blood. It is too advanced for us to cure. You have about six months to live, a year at most if you take radiation treatments and chemotherapy. You should get your affairs in order right away."

EVERY year thousands of patients hear their doctors give them the fateful prognosis and every year thousands of people die from illnesses such as cancer and AIDS. Some people diagnosed as terminally ill, however, do not die. Some live many years longer, some recover completely. Joyce Goetze is one of those. She regained her health and now, more than thirty years later, her children are grown and she continued her career in banking.

Why Don't Some Terminally Ill Patients Die?

Bernie Siegel, author of *Love, Medicine, and Miracles* and many other books, says when he first began to practice medicine he told patients the bad news about their terminal condition like doctors traditionally do. But every so often a person he had diagnosed as terminally ill would show up several years later. The person had fully recovered and was healthy. His prediction about this individual had been wrong.

Siegel began to wonder, "Why do we doctors always study dead people to see why they died? Why don't we study people who are still alive when they should be dead?"

He set out to find answers to his questions. He tracked down patients who had not died when physicians had predicted they should. He interviewed them. He listened. He learned from them.*

Siegel developed an understanding of survivors that is much like the picture my own research revealed. He found that differences in the way people react to major life threats affect whether they will recover. The question is, Why do some people recover from critical, seemingly hopeless conditions? What do survivors do that makes the difference?

Why Is Good Information So Scarce?

Answers to these questions about survival are not easy to find, however. The medical profession has devoted little attention to, and may even have avoided looking at, why some patients recover after physicians have decided they will die. Siegel came from an excellent medical school and was on staff at a highly regarded hospital. Yet when he became curious about people who didn't die as expected, he discovered that he had to do his own original research.

Physicians have a term for times when a person's illness disappears for no apparent reason. The term is *spontaneous remission*. If you ask a physician to tell you why some people recover after they are deemed to be beyond hope for a medical cure, the chances are you will not receive useful information.

The medical profession's lack of understanding about spontaneous remission is not because information about it does not exist. More than thirty years ago, psychiatrist W. C. Ellerbroek

---

*The references for this chapter are from Bernie Siegel's workshops and book *Love, Medicine, and Miracles*.

tried unsuccessfully for seven years to get medical journals to publish his paper about "how to keep yourself from getting cancer, or, if you have it, how to contribute to your own recovery." It was not until he rewrote his paper, titled "Language, Thought, and Disease," as though it were an article about acne that he was able to get it published in the minor journal *The Co-Evolution Quarterly*.

Researchers Caryle Hirshberg and Marc Barasch at the Institute of Noetic Sciences assembled the largest database on spontaneous remission in the world, but it took them many years to find a publisher willing to publish their book *Remarkable Recovery*.*

The Learning Challenge

It is not the purpose here to explore why the medical profession has not studied spontaneous remission from cancer and other illnesses. The purpose is to alert you that finding useful information includes overcoming a touchy subject with physicians. They have a professional blind spot about people who recover from supposedly terminal conditions.

Individuals wanting guidelines for survival when physicians are predicting they will die must develop their own survival strategy. The best way to sidestep physicians' pessimism is to interview people who have survived. Read survival accounts that include the inner story of what the person felt, thought, and chose to do.* *

---

*A copy of a short special report by Brendon O'Regan, the first director of research at the Institute of Noetic Sciences, titled "Healing, Remission, and Miracle Cures," is available online at www.FindArticles.com. The Noetic Sciences site is www.Noetic .org.
* *Several can be found at www.THRIVEnet.com; see also "Recommended Reading" on p. 223.

A Second Challenge

Another challenge in trying to understand what it takes to recover from a major illness or injury is that every individual's way of becoming a survivor is unique. Thus there is no direct transfer of how to do this from one person to another. There are no rules, no formulas, no recipes. What one person says worked for her will not necessarily fit with what you need to do, but perhaps you will be inspired to keep on searching and experimenting to discover what *is* right for you.

Barbara Brewster's recovery from multiple sclerosis included ending a dissatisfying marriage, giving up the small business she owned, and discovering and treating a yeast infection and mild allergies to many common foods. She also had to "change at other levels," she says, "to release outmoded habits, establish more wholesome behavior patterns, reorder my beliefs, turn inward, trust, and surrender to a higher power." In her book *Journey to Wholeness*, she says, "I had no idea how to do this or where the process would take me."

Barbara's way of recovering cannot be successfully repeated by anyone else because her life circumstances, her ways of thinking, the illness she developed, and the nature of her path to recovery were unique to her as it must be for anyone.

A Wake-Up Call

Siegel says that most patients who get better instead of dying react to their illness as a *wake-up call*. By that he means they make major changes in how they live, talk, think, feel, eat, and spend their time. In an article published in *Parade* magazine shortly after his heart attack, television talk show host Larry King wrote, "Until I had my coronary . . . I really think I had thought I was immortal. The shocking realization that I was close to dying was a brutal awakening to me. . . . A heart attack changes everything. You turn inward and think long and hard about what life means to you."

Individuals who change how they live, eat, think, and feel sometimes accomplish what seem to be miraculous recoveries. In 1975, Australian veterinarian Ian Gawler was training for the decathlon when he developed a swelling in his right leg. When the swelling did not go down, he consulted a doctor. He was found to have virulent bone cancer and had to have his leg amputated. Medical treatment did not halt the condition; tumors were appearing all over his body. In 1976, the physicians told him he had from three to six months to live.

Recounting his experience in his book *Peace of Mind*, Gawler says he searched for and began to practice "a whole range of things to stimulate the immune system." He meditated up to five hours a day. He went to healers. He started on an intensive dietary regimen. Fifteen months later, the tumors had completely disappeared—confirmed by a thorough medical workup.

Hey! I Have a Human Body!

Changes for someone who has almost died usually start with the realization that his or her body is not exempt from the laws of nature. Larry King says, "You have a heart attack. First thing you think is, 'I gotta change my life.' . . . If you smoke, you give up smoking. If you're a couch potato, you start exercising. If you live on steak, you switch to fish and broiled chicken." King, like others who get the wake-up call, stopped doing things that contribute to illness and started doing things that lead to improved health. The message here is that it is important to look at both sides of the recovery process because as Howard S. Friedman reports in *The Self-Healing Personality*, an understanding of self-managed healing is incomplete without an understanding of what humans do that is self-sickening.

A Self-Sickening Plan of Action

If you wanted to develop a serious or fatal illness on purpose, what would you do?

The response to this provocative question can tell you a lot about what predisposes a person to illness—and, conversely, what contributes to surviving and thriving.

Here are factors that commonly appear on lists from workshop participants of what a person could do to develop life-threatening illnesses:

- Be self-frazzling. Live a fast-paced, hectic life. Don't get adequate rest. Stay up late, get up early. Keep energized with caffeine.

- Eat fatty and salty foods. Drink beverages loaded with sugar. Avoid vegetables, fresh fruit, and whole grains.

- Smoke and drink frequently. Use tranquilizers and stimulants to control moods.

- Have unsafe sex with many partners. Shoot drugs with others, all using the same needle.

- Get angry with others but hide your feelings. Worry constantly. Feel unhappy but pretend to be happy.

- Get deeply into debt. Don't pay bills and become fearful whenever the phone rings or someone knocks on the door.

- Dislike your life and your relationships but do nothing to make any changes. Blame others for your unhappiness. Feel helpless and hopeless. Feel trapped. Count on winning the lottery as the solution to your difficulties.

This list of how to be self-sickening suggests that many people act as though they wanted to develop serious illnesses. They couldn't do a much better job of becoming sick if they tried on purpose.

Is it possible that excessive smoking, eating, drinking, and living a hectic, irritated life are a slow form of suicide? Possibly so, but there is another reason why people hang on to self-sickening actions and resist the efforts by others to get them to change. Information about how to live long, healthy lives is not part of our human knowledge base.

For thousands of years the saying "Eat, drink, and be merry for tomorrow we shall die" was a valid philosophy of life. It fit with how things were. The discovery that we humans have bodies designed for living in good health for more than a hundred years is a very recent development.

To live long, we have to create expectations different from humans of the past. Family histories, stories in books and plays, movies and television programs show most humans dying of diseases of old age in their sixties and seventies, if not earlier. Such images influence personal expectations. The expectations then become self-fulfilling. You believe something will happen so you live and act in such a way to bring it about.

Here are several questions to reflect on:

- How long do you expect to live? Is there a belief in your family about when most of you die?

- Do you want to live to be a hundred or more? What images come to mind if you imagine yourself being a hundred? Can you imagine yourself living an active, healthy, happy life at a hundred or more?

- Have you had negative reactions to someone trying to get you to change a lifestyle habit such as smoking, drinking, eating, or overworking? How important is it to prove to them that they can't *make* you change? Is it worth dying for?

Inner Changes Require Feeling and Thinking Differently

A long-time acquaintance of mine died of uterine cancer a while ago. She was a smiling, loving, New Age metaphysical counselor who tried every cancer treatment available, both traditional and nontraditional, with no positive results. When I suggested to her that there could be a relationship between the location of her cancer and having never expressed anger about being sexually molested by her stepfather when she was a girl, she explained that she felt only unqualified love for all humans, including her stepfather.

Perhaps there was no relationship in her case, but it is a quirk of human nature that when people develop afflictions, they often resist suggestions that they stop doing what apparently contributed to the affliction in the first place. The recovery challenge often boils down to whether the person will try doing the opposite of his or her well-practiced habit.

For a person raised to be good, the inner change may be to stop being so nice and start getting angry. Research in Europe presented by Hans J. Eysenk in the article "Health's Character" indicates that people who suppress angry feelings are more likely to get cancer, whereas people who are frequently angry with others are more likely to get heart attacks. For one person, the inner change is to be less tolerant and forgiving, to learn how to express angry feelings. For someone else, the change is to become more tolerant and forgiving, to learn how to give up the anger habit.

The reason for doing the opposite is to establish inner emotional balance. Every time you have a feeling, there is a corresponding neurochemical activity in your body. Lopsided habits in feelings and thoughts create matching imbalances in physical systems that make the body vulnerable to diseases and illnesses.

Many people mistakenly believe their identity is wrapped up in their thoughts and habits. They think they wouldn't be themselves if they gave up some mental and emotional habits they learned as children. For the person raised to be a good child, for example, learning healthy self-love is difficult even though almost everyone working in the healing arts emphasizes the importance of self-love in people with serious problems or illnesses.

Self-love is essential for overcoming the fear of not being loved by others when you drop old, energy-draining habits. Self-love has to be strong enough to support the thinking that you deserve a happier, healthier life. It takes self-love to be motivated to work for a better life, one that supports your well-being.

Ed Roberts, who spent much of his life in an iron lung, played a major role in getting the state of California to create the Centers of Independent Living for persons with disabilities. In an interview in *This Brain Has a Mouth*, he recounted that the long, difficult struggle started when he was a student at the University of California at Berkeley in the 1960s. He said that the people involved in creating the first Independent Living Center on campus were "a whole bunch of people with progressive disabilities like multiple sclerosis, muscular dystrophy, people whose disability was terminal. They got involved in the politics of independent living and they lived longer—not one or two years, but fifteen or twenty."

Roberts, who was later appointed director of the Department of Rehabilitation for the state of California, said in the interview, "People who are going, who are motivated, don't get sick as much."

Sometimes the internal shift that leads to recovery may be to become less dedicated to helping others. Anne Seitz was thirty-nine years old, happily married, and the mother of four young sons when she went to her doctor for a routine physical checkup. She thought it was unusual to have to go back a second time for extra tests but assumed the doctor was just being thorough.

When she went to his office to find out the results, she became anxious when she saw the sullen look on his face. She told me, "I had to grab the arms of my chair and hold on tight to keep from fainting when he said I had ovarian cancer. He said no operation or treatment could save me and, at most, I had a year to live. He told me to tie up my loose ends."

Outside in her car she broke down and sobbed. She loved her husband. She loved her sons. She didn't want to leave them. After a while she sat up and took a deep breath. She said to herself, "If I have to die young, I'm going to enjoy what's left of my life while I'm here!" On the way home she stopped at a market and bought fresh lobster tails for dinner. She made her family their favorite dessert.

A few days later Anne decided, "If I have only one more year with my family, it is going to be the best year of our lives." She stopped going to meetings. She said no to invitations. She stopped all activities that were not something enjoyable to do with her husband and sons. That was in 1971. Decades later, she told me she was enjoying her three grandchildren and that her "life continues to improve, considerably, with age."

Anne did not devote herself to having happy times with her family for the purpose of getting rid of the cancer. Regaining her health was an unexpected outcome of having wonderful times with them every day.

For Anne, getting rid of the illness was not the goal. Her recovery resulted from making positive changes in her life. To try to make your body not be sick is a negative goal. Any negative goal, such as trying to stop smoking, or to not be sick, is difficult to reach. A positive goal is learning to do what is good for your health and well-being.

Self-Managed Healing

It would be useful here to comment on the title chosen for this chapter. Even though *self-healing* is a more commonly used phrase, I disagree that anyone actually heals himself or herself. What a person does is make a change that facilitates healing. Anne Seitz did not intend to heal herself. What she did was change her life in a way that led to her tumors disappearing. The term *self-managed healing* thus gives us a wider perspective. It can encompass any recovery occurring after deciding to live a better-quality life and making the changes. The healing can occur whether intended or not, whether due to inner thoughts or outer lifestyle.

The Change May Be to Become Defiant

Joyce Goetze told me that after she learned that the boils breaking out on her body were symptoms of leukemia, she went into the hospital for chemotherapy. She stayed thirty-three days. After one week off, she went back for chemotherapy again. She says:

> I felt upset and angry. I was raised a Catholic. I wondered, "What have I done? Why am I being punished by God?"
>
> My parents took me to the coast as often as I wanted. I felt tired but I wanted to walk on the beach with my children. Just walking was tiring, but I'd push myself. Sometimes I'd sit and watch the waves. I'd cry, cry until I was dry, no more tears. When I came home, I'd sleep for many hours. My father kept saying to not tire myself.
>
> After a few weeks I could see how the doctors and my parents were limiting me, restricting me. The doctors were telling me when I would die, my parents were telling me that they would raise my children. I was raised to obey my father, he was strict with us. The doctors saw hundreds of patients, they were the experts. They had done this hundreds of times, but it was the first time for me. They were talking to me like I was a statistic. But they didn't see it was *me* with leukemia. I didn't like how they talked to me. I'm not a statistic. I'm me.
>
> I kept thinking of having only a year or less to live. I saw it was what the doctors believed. The doctors were restricting

how long I could live. I decided to take a stand. I put my foot
down. I decided I was going to be in control. I decided I was
going to handle this. It was a long shot, but I was going to
take it. I didn't have to let the doctors and my parents limit
how long I could live.

I went to the beach whenever I could. I really pushed
myself emotionally. I felt like the rubber ball on a paddle ball.
I told myself again and again I didn't want to die, didn't want
someone else raising my children, I wanted to raise them
myself. I pushed the limits. I turned everything inside out,
upside down, backwards, and reverse. I pushed myself to the
limits to gain control over my emotions and my life.

I cried, and when I couldn't cry anymore, I'd roll in the
sand laughing. I must have looked crazy to people walking
by. I'm five feet three inches and my weight was only sixty-
five pounds. My clothes hung on me like robes. I lost all my
hair. You couldn't tell if I was a man or a woman. I wore a
scarf or a cap on my head. When the wind blew, it could
almost blow me away. Here is this strange looking skinny
person sitting by the ocean crying and laughing. I set no
goals, just kept going one day at a time.

Then one day in the spring, about eight or nine months
after I was first in the hospital, my father was bringing me
home from chemotherapy. It was a sunny day, flowers were
blooming. I suddenly knew I was in control of the leukemia;
it was not in control of me. I knew I had control over it.

I kept on day after day, week after week, until the year
was out. By the end of summer I was still alive and getting
stronger. The chemotherapy upset me. I didn't like it. You
can't eat—or if you do, you throw up. But I knew I had to do

it and got used to it. My doctor was surprised. He scratched his head. He couldn't explain why I was still alive, but he said, "Go for it."

I went to chemotherapy for two years before I stopped. The oncology doctors told me the leukemia would be in remission for one, two, or three years and then come back. I told them to not restrict me with their talk of three years. I told them to never talk to me that way.

Survivors Are Not Good Patients

Bernie Siegel discovered that people who recover from advanced stages of cancer are often described by the hospital staff as *difficult patients*. He says that when he consults on a case, he likes to see entries in the patient's hospital chart that the patient is "uncooperative," "questions why tests are ordered," "demands to be told about test results," and "insists on explanations about treatments."

These difficult patients ask why other treatments are not being used or may insist that the physician try something different. They are patients with an attitude. It is an attitude that they are in charge of themselves, not the physician. This is not an attitude that many physicians handle well.

Who Is to Say What Is Impossible for You?

From Feldenkrais practitioners I learned how Moshe Feldenkrais had a badly damaged knee from years of playing soccer and competing in the martial arts. Physicians told him that his chances of saving his lower leg with surgery were about fifty-

fifty. He didn't like the odds. Moshe, a physicist, reasoned that because the human body can heal and repair itself, he would help his knee do that. He studied books on anatomy and physiology to learn the precise structure and function of every muscle in his leg and hip. He then created and practiced a series of small, pain-free, frequently repeated movements designed to rebuild the neuromuscular connections and patterns. He succeeded and went on to teach others how to use the methods he pioneered. Many people find additional physical relief from pain by combining the Feldenkrais method with Pilates.

The Cure Is More in Taking Responsibility Than in the Specific Treatment

Most people have heard how the late Norman Cousins, the long-time editor of *Saturday Review*, used laughter to help himself recover from a fatal disease. When I ask people about the lesson to be learned from his story, they usually say, "Laughing is good for you." For me, however, the important lesson is in the way Cousins reacted when physicians told him he was dying.

In August 1964, Cousins had become critically ill. He could move only with great difficulty. He underwent extensive medical tests. He reported in his book *Anatomy of an Illness* that there was:

> A consensus that I was suffering from a serious collagen illness—a disease of the connective tissue. . . . Collagen is the fibrous substance that binds cells together. In a sense, then, I was becoming unstuck. I had considerable difficulty in moving my limbs and even in turning over in bed. Nodules appeared on my body, gravel-like substances under the skin,

indicating the systemic nature of the disease. At the low point of my illness, my jaws were almost locked.

The pain in his body was so severe he was not able to sleep. Specialists called in on his case found that the connective tissue in his spine was disintegrating also. Cousins asked his doctor about his chances for full recovery. "He leveled with me, admitting that one of the specialists had told him I had one chance in five hundred. The specialist had also stated that he had not personally witnessed a recovery from this comprehensive condition."

How did Cousins react? He said, "All this gave me a great deal to think about. Up to that time, I had been more or less disposed to let the doctors worry about my condition. But now I felt a compulsion to get into the act. It seemed clear to me that if I was to be that one in five hundred, I had better be something more than a passive observer."

He started asking questions. His search for information about how people recover from terminal conditions led him to vitamin C and the laughing cure. He decided that the hospital was not a good place for getting well. He checked out and moved into a hotel room. He borrowed videotapes of *Candid Camera* programs and obtained old Charlie Chaplin films. He found that after an hour of hearty laughing he could fall asleep and get the rest he needed. He gradually recovered his health, and went on to write and speak about the value of laughter.

The Doctor–Patient Puzzle

Differences in how patients and physicians react to each other is a thorny puzzle to unravel. Some physicians speak in ways that discourage patients and make them give up hope. Cousins, on the other hand, in writing about his illness and his recovery, says, "If I had to guess, I would say that the principal contribution made by my doctor to the taming, and possibly the conquest, of my illness was that he encouraged me to believe I was a respected partner with him in the total undertaking. He fully engaged my subjective energies."

On the other hand, when Bernie Siegel announced the beginning of a support group where people with cancer could learn how to live better and longer, he got a big surprise. He says he sent out a hundred letters. He assumed people with cancer would tell others and word would spread. He says "I began to get nervous about how to handle the crowd that would appear."

How many showed up? Twelve.

Siegel says it was then that he started to learn there are three kinds of patients. He estimates that 15 to 20 percent at some level of consciousness wish to die and will do so no matter how excellent their treatment. Between 60 and 70 percent passively cooperate with whatever the physicians say. They want an authority to tell them what to do, and they cooperate fully, including dying when the physicians predict. But 15 to 20 percent are the exceptional patients. They refuse to be cancer victims or let their physicians discourage them. It was for this latter kind of person that Siegel founded the national network of groups for Exceptional Cancer Patients (ECaP) because most hospitals and physicians did not support the spirit of uncooperative patients.*

---

*For more information, see www.ECaP-Online.org.

Who Is in Control?

The puzzle begins to unravel as we explore two significant ways in which physicians and patients differ from each other. Sometimes the differences in physicians and patients are beneficial, sometimes they are an upsetting mismatch.

Many physicians become irritated with patients who won't obediently follow instructions and who won't accept that the doctor's prognosis is accurate for them. Such physicians are not usually open to considering information about alternative treatments brought to them by patients or relatives. Other physicians, however, appreciate having a patient who asks questions, wants explanations, suggests treatment changes, and is active in creating a recovery plan.

On the patient's side, the majority want to be told what to do by a doctor. They do not seek or want to hear advice about what they can do on their own. Other patients, however, become defiant with physicians who expect patients to do as they are told.

Some people believe they are controlled by outside forces, that they are pawns of fate. Others feel responsible for whatever happens in their lives—their health or sickness, their successes or failures.

Psychologists refer to this personality variable as the "internal-external locus of control." Bonnie Strickland, in her presidential address to the American Psychological Association, said that people with a high external locus of control respond well to placebos. When the physician says the medicine or treatment will work, even if it is a sugar pill, the person usually gets better. On the other hand, people with a high internal locus of control do not respond to placebos. They ask for proof. They do not respond well to a physician saying, "Take this" without explaining how and why it will work or why this medicine is better than another.

So we have a situation in which the very same words and attitude emotionally supportive for one patient prove alienating to another.

As shown in the diagram below, a physician with an authoritarian or paternalistic style is a poor match with an internal locus of control individual who may be infuriated by a doctor who gives Simon Says commands to patients. But the same physician is a good match for an external locus of control patient who needs to have an authority in control of what is done.

In contrast, a physician with a participative, open-minded style is a good match for someone similar to Norman Cousins who had

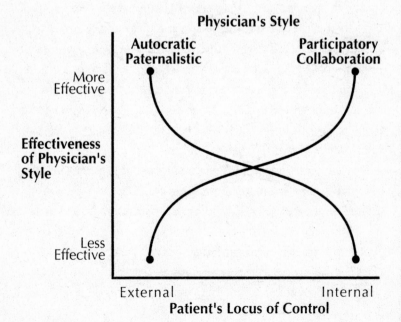

a strong internal locus of control. Yet this same physician may be a poor match with an external locus of control patient.

High external patients do not want to be given choices, told about probabilities, asked questions about why the illness developed at this time, or made to feel guilty because they do not have the desire to transform their lives. Certified Insurance Rehabilitation Specialist William Meagher explained to me that they want a doctor to tell them what medicine and treatments to take. For example, a while after that conversation, I saw a secretary from a local college limping across the street. When I inquired about what had happened, she said she had developed a nerve disease in her legs and arms. As we talked I asked if she was doing anything on her own to recover her health. I said, "I know of some resources, if you are interested."

"No," she said, "my doctor told me that lots of people will give me advice but I'm not to listen. He is in charge of my treatment. I'll do what he says."

Being Both Internal and External

The paradoxical tendencies found in survivors hold true with the internal-external locus of control as well. Joy Blitch knew that the large masses growing in her chest were not normal. A religious woman, she prayed for good health, but the masses kept growing. When she finally agreed to let her husband take her for a medical examination, the doctors said the masses were too large and that her condition was inoperable. They told her she had only a few days to live.

"I cried my eyes out for a week," she said, "and cried myself to sleep because I believed the specialist who said I had one week to live. I even made all the arrangements for my funeral!"

Joy stayed in the hospital, but even though she refused chemotherapy and radiation treatments, she did not die as expected. The doctors told her not to walk around because that would spread the cancer cells in her body. They advised her against talking much and told her that visitors would upset her. She said:

> I prayed to God for guidance. . . . I somehow knew there were too many things unfinished in my life, that I had important work to do. I wanted to raise my son and see him grow up. I wanted to continue working with my husband in our home-based business. I had important Christian work to do.
>
> After five months of lying in bed, not being around people, not walking, and all the other things the doctors had me not doing, I decided if I acted as though I were well, instead of sick, I just might get well. Then I programmed myself constantly, "It is not what the doctors believe, it is what I believe that counts!"

"One by one, the things they had told me started not counting in my mind." The change was not instantaneous. "I had to work at each thing by itself," she said. "First I ignored the 'don't talk out loud' instruction. Then 'don't be around any people,' 'stay in bed' and, finally, 'don't walk much.'"

A year later, she was back home. She went walking every day and talked with people as much as she wished. Joy still had the tumors, but she believed from reading the Bible that if she could find a minister to perform the healing ritual, God would heal her completely. She said, "My own minister wouldn't do it. I showed him the passage in the Bible but he turned me down. I went to other ministers but they wouldn't do the ritual. I telephoned many churches. I finally found a minister in Chicago who knew about the ritual and said he would perform it for me over the telephone."

Joy said that immediately after the ritual the tumors started to shrink. Several months later, they were completely gone. "My doctor was amazed," she said, "he checked his records but found he hadn't made a mistake. I kept telling him it was God's will for me not to die."

Joy started telling her story to friends. She spoke about her recovery at business conferences. People from all over the country would telephone her late at night and early in the morning to ask her for help. She lost sleep. She tried to help everyone who contacted her. She wrote letters. She prayed for a long list of people. She talked on the phone for hours.

Then her tumors reappeared. She prayed for health but they got larger. She went to the doctor again. He said her condition was incurable. She had the minister in Chicago do another healing ritual and again the tumors disappeared.

This time she started saying no to most people requesting help. She no longer answered her phone during the night. She spent more time with her son and husband. About five years later, the tumors reappeared, but her prayers and the healing ritual were not able to make them go away the third time.

Joy's way of reacting to the physicians' beliefs about her was to use an internal style to transfer control over her recovery from one external authority to another. She replaced her acceptance of the physicians' authority in such matters with her belief in God's power.

Spiritual Healing and Nonspiritual Healing

Keep in mind that Blitch had been expected to die at the end of the week—yet she confounded the experts by living for many more years. Such astonishing cases are not that rare. The Christian Science church has thousands of testimonials from people healed through "spiritual-mindedness," a healing method "based solely on the healing power of God, not of the human mind."

At Lourdes, in France, at the sight where an apparition of the Virgin Mary appeared in 1858, there have been over six thousand miraculous healings registered. (Sixty-seven of these have passed the stringent scrutiny of the International Medical Commission and have been officially declared miracles.)

Yet while many people are healed through a spiritual experience, there are many nonbelievers who experience healings. A man I know, an outspoken agnostic, has healed himself twice of cancer. Both times he used meditation and imagination in ways taught by Carl Simonton and Stephanie Mathews-Simonton.

Healing: Can You Imagine That?

Carl Simonton, an oncologist, and Stephanie Matthews-Simonton, a psychologist, have developed imaging techniques with impressive results even with cancer patients diagnosed as having medically incurable malignancies. As reported in their classic book *Getting Well Again with James L. Creighton*, about 9 percent of the patients using imaginative processes got rid of their cancer completely, 8 percent had the cancer regressing, and 11 percent had stabilized the disease. Altogether, the 159 patients in their first program lived roughly twice as long as other patients with similar conditions.

In 1974, the tumor in the center of John Evans's back was diagnosed as a malignant melanoma. The cancer was also found in his lymph nodes. John was told that even with extensive surgery the odds were ten to one against his surviving even for five years.

John's reaction was "I am not a statistic. I am a living, breathing, thinking, human organism. And as a unique individual, despite any highly abstract odds against me, I have at any given moment at least a fifty-fifty chance. My choice is that my life is to 'go' rather than 'no-go!'" He then contacted Carl Simonton by phone. John says Simonton encouraged him to develop his own imaging technique while following his physician's orders, and to use creative mental imaging as an adjunct to medical treatment, not a substitute for it.

As told to me and reported in "Imagination Therapy," an article in *The Humanist*, the mental imagery that John used while undergoing the surgeries was to imagine "my white blood cells were huge white hunting dogs, with an uncanny sense of smell. My hunting dogs would sniff around and flush out cancer cells that might be hiding. The cancer cells were small, nuisance rodents which, when flushed, would be attacked by the dogs. A dog would grab and break its neck. I could then picture the dead and dying cells being sloughed off."

For each person the image has to be one he or she subjectively feels is powerful and effective. For this reason, it may not work well to be told what to imagine. It works best for each person to invent what he or she feels could be an effective cancer destroyer.

Healing by Changing Self-Talk

One difficulty with recommending images is that approximately half of all people cannot consciously create mental pictures. Telling them to create mental images only frustrates them. Fortunately, changing your way of thinking about the illness and your self-talk can also have a healing effect.

John Evans overcame his cancer, earned an EdD in general semantics and counseling, and now teaches people how to think and talk about their illnesses in ways that promote healing. He promotes writing about your experience. He teaches people with illnesses to stop asking, Why did this happen to me? and just describe what is happening. He teaches them to replace the question *Why do I have this illness?* with the statement *I have this illness.* He says "once clients can throw away the 'why me?' question they are on the road to self-help."*

Louise Hay, author of *You Can Heal Your Life*, finds that it can be very useful for a person to search for answers to questions such as:

- Why this illness at this time?

- Who do you need to forgive?

- What is the truth that needs to be told?

- What is happening in your life at this time?

- Are you happy?

---

*For more information on using writing to help you with your own healing, see John's website, www.WellnessAndWritingConnections.com.

- What is your body telling you?

- What problem does this illness resolve?

Hay, a social worker by training, teaches that "the only thing we are ever dealing with is a thought, and a thought can be changed." As an example, the support group she started years ago for people with AIDS had to change its name to the PLWA group, for People *Living* with AIDS. She learned through interactions with survivors that their way of viewing their condition is to see that being HIV positive is like having any other chronic infection, and an infection can be treated and lived with. This is proving to be the case. Many people in her support group who developed AIDS have become long-term survivors, and many who are HIV positive never develop full-blown AIDS.

Information about the connection between thoughts, words, and illness has existed for many years, although it did not receive popular attention until recently. Many years ago, psychiatrist W. C. Ellerbroek wrote in "Hypotheses Toward a Unified Theory of Human Behavior," an article that appeared in *Perspectives in Biology and Medicine*, that "a 'disease' is managed by all the specific psycholinguistic and behavioral events in the life history" of a person and the entire field of the person's life experiences. Ellerbroek argued that "since postures, voices, behaviors, words, and thoughts are all modifiable behaviors—there is therefore no such thing as an untreatable disease."

His way of working with patients included teaching them, first, to describe their disease or illness as a behavior. For example, he taught them to replace saying "I have the measles" with "I am measling." Second, he taught his patients to accept whatever was happening as being exactly the way things should be.

Any illness or condition, he emphasized, is an effect of everything that has happened in a person's life and in the world.

There is much more to Ellerbroek's method of how to regain health than can be included here. The point is that changing your words, thoughts, and self-talk can have an amazingly positive effect.

Self-Talk Can Be Overdone

While many of the current teachings about self-healing emphasize the power of prayer, positive self-talk, and imagination, none of them indicate that trying too hard can be self-defeating. Emile Coué observed that repeating "Day by day, in every way, I am getting better and better" over and over can have very positive effects on health, finances, and relationships. Coué opened a free clinic, and through his teachings helped thousands of people regain health and improve their lives. Couéism spread to the United States and became a popular movement in the 1920s.

As John Duckworth quotes in his book *How to Use Auto-Suggestion Effectively*, Coué said the effect of his incantation/mantra/affirmation worked best when it was repeated passively and casually—without thinking about it much. Why so? To avoid the law of reversed effort. Coué discovered that strong conscious effort, what is often called *willpower*, can trigger an opposite, defeating effect. Conscious, forceful willing can create a reverse thought in imagination. Declaring "I will get well!" may be followed by a tiny voice in your imagination that says, "Are you sure?" or "What if you don't?" According to Coué, "When the will and the imagination are in conflict, the imagination invariably wins the day."

There Is No Right Way—Just the Best Way for You

If you expect that you can get better, then doing anything you feel will be helpful will probably get better results than doing something you hope might be helpful just because others have said it is. The power seems to be more in doing what you feel and believe is right for you, than in the specific method itself.

Some individuals who develop severe cancerous conditions, such as the late Paul Pearsall, author of books on joyous living such as *Making Miracles: A Scientist's Journey to Death and Back*, devote themselves completely to the treatments. They combine the best that medical science has to offer with prayer and family support. Others, such as a professional gardener seen by Bernie Siegel, walk away saying, "I don't have time to go into the hospital," and they recover.

The Medical Profession Is Learning

If you are ill, the most important step for survival may be to find a physician who supports your survival spirit. Your chances of finding such a physician are greater than in the past because the medical profession is giving more attention to what health and regaining health are all about. Healthcare professionals have, in fact, become more willing to study the relationship between feelings, thinking, and health because they finally have a term for the subject that laymen can hardly pronounce. The term is psychoneuroimmunology (PNI).

Norman Cousins was appointed to the medical school faculty at UCLA and organized conferences on PNI. His book *Head*

First: The Biology of Hope provides an easily accessible account of the many new ways that physicians and hospitals are giving patients emotional support and creating better healing environments. In it, for example, he reports that many hospitals now have "laughing rooms" that play comedy videos.

Scientific studies into the relationship between the mind and disease have made the mind–body connection an important part of modern medical education. More physicians are recognizing the role that an individual's survival spirit plays. A woman told me recently that when she was diagnosed with cancer, her physician said, "Whether you live or die is up to you. I can treat the cancer, but you will determine if the treatment is successful or not."

Physicians who want to treat the whole person, not just the illness, have formed a national network of physicians practicing holistic medicine. At their conferences they include sessions for learning how to set an example by living a more healthy lifestyle themselves.*

Many hospitals have built care centers devoted to treating chronic disease conditions that include addressing patients' mental health needs and developing opportunities for family and friends to become involved in the treatment process.

Programs now exist that create conditions conducive to spontaneous remission. They often promote activities such as laughing, juggling, playing, meditating, painting, journaling, exercising, and eating nutritiously. (Searching the Internet will yield dozens of results.) Deirdre Brigham, founder and director of the former Getting Well program in Florida, once told me, "It is uncanny.

---

*For more information, see the American Holistic Medical Association website at www.HolisticMedicine.org.

When you see someone come in you may think 'no way' can this person recover, yet many terminally ill people in our program become healthier and go into spontaneous remission. And the ones who don't recover, do get healthier, have a shorter decline, and die more quickly and peacefully." Her book *Imagery for Getting Well*, based on her twenty-eight-step program, discusses mind–body strategies she found valuable toward regaining health during chronic illness.

The point here is that if you don't like the way one physician or therapist talks to you, ask for another—just as you would with any person providing a service you are paying for. Most important, it is vital to associate with people who help you maintain your spirit and help you feel loved.

Guidance and Inspiration from Survivors

Individuals who have survived and overcome extreme physical difficulties often become a source of learning and encouragement for others. Helen Keller was deaf and blind from the age of two. Through her teacher, Anne Sullivan, she learned Braille, how to speak, and how to understand what people were saying when she put her fingers on their lips. She was an eager student. Years later she graduated with honors from Radcliffe College. During World War II, Keller worked with blinded soldiers, giving them hope and courage.

Author Dorothy Woods Smith had polio as a child. She worked for years to strengthen her legs and learned to walk without braces. Many years later, after becoming a nurse, educator, and consultant, she developed post-polio problems. She had muscle spasms in her back and pains in her lower back and legs. She had to draw on her years of experience to recover.

She now writes articles about recovery from what healthcare professionals may inaccurately believe is a hopeless, debilitating condition. She has "created a community of healers to bridge the gap between conventional medicine and complementary healing practices." She talks to physically challenged people about "giving up the false comfort of magical thinking, no longer empowering the doctor, nurse, and therapist to make our choices for us, and learning instead to join with health care professionals as partners."

John Callahan become an alcoholic by the age of twelve, and was paralyzed in a car accident shortly after his twenty-first birthday. In his book *Don't Worry, He Won't Get Far on Foot*, Callahan describes himself as "a C5-6 quadriplegic . . . I can extend my fingers, but not close them around a fork or a pen."

After six years of heavy drinking, Callahan says he realized his problem "was not quadriplegia but alcoholism." With his recovery, he returned to his childhood passion of drawing cartoons. He can't move all his fingers, so he draws cartoons by clutching a pen in his right hand and guiding it across the page with his left.

John Callahan's cartoons are now internationally syndicated. He has several cartoon books in print, two animated series on TV, and a line of greeting cards, calendars, mugs, T-shirts, and more.

The Unexpected Benefit of Self-Managed Healing: A Stronger Life Spirit

Although the original goal of self-managed healing may be to get over an illness or injury, something else often happens. As in the examples given in this chapter, by taking control of your own healing, your life spirit too can emerge stronger than before. It may be in a new direction or with a new purpose, but life's best survivors embrace the change and often report finding a gift in their tragedy. Before finding the gift, however, you must survive the event.

TWELVE

Surviving Emergencies and Crises

Facing emergencies can be especially challenging because of the shock and unexpectedness involved. Often survival may hinge upon taking effective actions before one has fully absorbed what is happening.

The Survivor Style

When award-winning photojournalist Alison Wright was in a harrowing bus–truck collision on a winding jungle road in Laos, she found herself profusely bleeding with a shattered arm, unable to move around, and—most alarming—having difficulty breathing due to collapsed lungs and diaphragm. By relying entirely on her upper body strength, she managed to pull herself out of the wreckage and onto the side of the road. "In the distance," she says, "I could hear muffled voices calling, 'My God, someone do something! This woman is bleeding to death.'" She says she prayed that someone would help the woman, then quickly realized that the woman they were talking about was her.

The pain soon came. Drawing on her years of meditation and yoga practice, Alison knew to go within herself to find strength. "I believe that having this skill, this tool, is what helped me not just survive but also got me through the subsequent healing," she says.

It took fourteen hours, two stops, and many miles over jarring roads for her to receive anything close to advanced medical attention. At the first stop in a small village, she had her arm sewn up. When she learned that a helicopter would not be able to fly her out that night, she says she had a moment of clarity that she was probably going to die. With this acceptance, she was able to let go of all her fears and surrendered to her suffering. She says a calm came over her, the pain was gone, and she was "ready to go." She said that she had a near-death experience that brought to her visions of the interconnectedness of the universe, and the overpowering sense of love—things she hadn't really noticed before—that added to her inner resolve. Meanwhile, she continued to focus on her breathing and against all odds, survived the final part of the journey on to Thailand.

At the hospital in Udon Thani, Alison learned she had a broken back, pelvis, and ribs and extreme internal injuries. She had a herniated heart and a ruptured spleen, her diaphragm was punctured, and her lungs were filling up with fluid. Alison flat-lined just as she was being anesthetized for surgery and was revived by the one surgeon working in the hospital at the time.

Throughout her ordeal, Alison had the self-control to keep her mind in a place of inner peace. She succeeded and survived because she focused on survival. At times her brain blocked out her pain and allowed her to do whatever she had to do to not die on a rural Laotian road, including later giving herself the permission to let go and accept death. This required her to adapt and develop new survival strategies and attitudes several times, under the worst of conditions. Her intention to survive, and even her willingness to let go, never wavered.

Ordinary People in Extraordinary Circumstances

It is common for people to think of someone like Alison as an extraordinary person, that the average person would not have done so well. But Alison, as do most survivors, knows that she is an ordinary person who was forced to cope with an extreme situation.

The question is, what makes it possible for an ordinary person to survive an extraordinary life crisis?

The answer, I believe, is that a survivor style results from interacting with everyday life in ways that increase the probability of survival when survival is necessary. In her book *Learning to Breathe: One Woman's Journey of Spirit and Survival*, Alison recounts how various prior experiences of hers all prepared her to face this situation, though, taken individually, none of them was particularly exceptional.

In other words, your habitual way of reacting to everyday events influences your chances of being a survivor in a crisis or an emergency. It is an interaction style based on using inborn potentials that you can re-access and develop rather than acting necessarily as you've been taught. The style includes three basic elements:

- Quickly absorb information about what is happening.

- Expect that something can be done to influence events in a way that leads to a good outcome.

- Be willing to consider using *any* possible action or reaction.

Because of their life-long curiosity, people with survivor personalities react to a surprising incident or unexpected development by wondering what is going on: What is this? What's happening? Their automatic openness to absorb new information epitomizes the survivor orientation. It characterizes their response to the world under normal circumstances as well as unusual ones. Whether going for a walk or reacting to an emergency, they are alert to external circumstances, events, facts, or developments.

Discover Your Survivor Strengths and Weaknesses

Author Ben Sherwood, along with Dr. Courtney McCashland and her organization TalentMine, a psychological testing firm, created an online assessment tool for his book *The Survivors Club: The Secrets and Science That Could Save Your Life* to help you discover your survivor style.*

After many interviews with survivors, Sherwood came to believe that knowing your strengths and weaknesses ahead of time can allow you to build on what you have and work at what

---

*The assessment, known as the Survivor Profiler, is available at www.TheSurvivorsClub.org.

you may be lacking. McCashland used her experience, honed at the Gallup polling organization, to determine five basic types of survivors:

- **The Fighter.** Competitive, tenacious, meets adversity head on.

- **The Believer.** Optimistic, confident, puts faith in God or a greater power.

- **The Connector.** Empathetic, networker, draws strength from relationships.

- **The Thinker.** Analytical, creative, sees challenges clearly.

- **The Realist.** Calm, pragmatic, goes with the flow.

Each type has attached to it a mix of twelve personality traits, or tools, including adaptability, faith, tenacity, intelligence, instinct, and flow, that are most commonly found in survivors and that have the greatest influence on survivable situations. While Sherwood admits that it may be simplistic to lump all of humanity into five categories and twelve traits, the assessment has proved to be quite accurate and useful. Sherwood goes on to explain that, although it is not common to be able to change your survivor style, you can work at developing the traits that you score the lowest on.

Faster Than Words

One of the most important traits is the ability to adapt to new realities quickly. It is difficult to write about how to question, assess, decide, and act rapidly because the sequence happens faster than words. The questions remain unverbalized. Possible outcomes of several alternatives are weighed against one another, and action is taken so quickly that the whole sequence seems to be a reflex. This can occur in fractions of a second.

A workshop participant related the following incident to me:

I was driving out of the city one afternoon thinking about my work. I was at a place where the highway goes under an overpass. Off to my left I noticed a man racing down the embankment on the other side of the road.

He looked desperate. He was looking back over his shoulder behind him. He ran straight across the traffic lanes between the cars and I knew he wasn't going to stop at the median barrier. I knew he didn't see me and that I couldn't avoid hitting him even if I stepped on the brakes.

I stepped on the gas and swerved into the emergency lane. He jumped the median barrier the way I knew he would and, still looking back over his shoulder, came across the lanes running at full speed. I don't know how I got past him, but I did, and I swear he didn't miss my left rear fender by more than a foot and a half. I stopped the car when I could and walked back. By that time, the police had him in custody. They told me he had just robbed a store.

This driver was amazed at how rapidly and accurately he had read the situation. In a split second, he was able to take evasive action without thinking about what he was doing. He reacted in an automatic way and did the right thing.

His experience was not that unusual, however. Athletes in competitive sports such as football, soccer, and basketball do the same thing all the time. The best athletes read the play, process the information, and take effective action in a fraction of a second.

Fast Questioning Expands Awareness and Develops Action Choices

The quick scan of a critical situation usually includes a fast reading of what other people are perceiving, feeling, and doing. The ability to take in information rapidly might be called accelerated learning or high-speed curiosity.

This quick grasp of the total circumstance is a type of pattern empathy. The survivor style is to quickly read reality and simultaneously reach for the best action or reaction from your toolbox of paradoxical resources. This automatic and sometimes unconscious process can cause the individual to later be astonished by what he's done, and to wonder just how he accomplished it.

In a crisis, the survivor reflex is to rapidly ask unverbalized clusters of questions, such as:

- What is happening? Not happening?

- Should I jump, duck, grab, yell, freeze, or what?

- How much time do I have? How little?

- Must I do anything? Nothing?

- What are others doing? Not doing? Why?

- Where do I fit in the scene?

- Have I been noticed? How do I appear in their eyes?

- How are others reacting? What are their feelings?

- How serious is this?

- How much danger exists now? Is it over?

- Does anyone need help? Who doesn't?

The more quickly a person grasps the total picture of what is happening, the better his chance for survival. Anger, fear, and panic narrow what a person sees and reduce awareness.

Truck drivers, for example, know that they are more likely to have an accident when they are angry with an automobile driver. When they get angry with a driver for squeezing in front of them, they lose awareness of what is happening in traffic farther up ahead.

Insurance company records show that people going through separations and divorces are high accident risks. A driver who is angry, upset, or preoccupied loses awareness of the road and other drivers. Those involved in cell phone or texting conversations can be just as bad. The evidence is clear on this point. These mental states can result in driving behaviors and reaction times as dangerous as if you were under the influence of drugs or alcohol. Being calm, alert, and aware of what is around you decreases accidents; strong emotions and external distractions inhibit that awareness.

Alertness, pattern recognition, empathy, and awareness can be viewed as a sort of open-brainedness. This open-brainedness is a mental orientation that does not impose preexisting patterns on new information, but rather allows new information to reshape a person's mental maps. A person who has the best chance of handling a situation well is usually one with the best mental maps, pictures, or images of what is occurring outside of the body. In contrast, those people who are not able to survive well on their own tend to have inaccurate or distorted mental constructions of what is happening in the world around them.

At this moment your brain is being fed electrochemical impulses from activities occurring at your sense receptors and sense organs. Various energies are hitting your body carrying information about what is happening in the surrounding world. People with a survivor style are, apparently, the best at constructing an accurate internal representation of the outside world in their brains.

In contrast, those people who are not able to survive well, if left to their own devices, tend to have incorrect or distorted constructions of what is happening in the world outside their bodies. When you listen to some people talk and watch what they do—how they act, think, feel, and describe things—it becomes clear that their perceptions do not match well with what is actually going on in the world. Their quick emotional reactions tend to overwhelm their cerebral cortexes and/or have them jumping to inaccurate conclusions about what is going on.

To Survive an Emergency: Stay Calm

What can you do in highly emotional moments? Take some combination of these actions:

- Tell yourself to stay calm.

- Take a deep breath and relax.

- Repeat a saying.

- See something amusing about the moment, if possible.

Telling yourself to stay calm and relax is a useful reflex. Several deep breaths will help. Blind rage, screaming, panic, or fainting are not good solutions to a crisis unless done out of choice as a way to affect others.

In his book *How to Be Rich*, oilman billionaire John Paul Getty gave as his number one rule for dealing with a crisis:

> No matter what happens, do not panic. The panic-stricken individual cannot think or act effectively. A certain amount of trouble is inevitable in any business career—when it comes, it should be met with calm determination.

To illustrate, in early 1995 a seventeen-year-old girl living in Oakland, California, purchased her first car. It was a used Oldsmobile. She felt very proud of it. That evening she wanted to drive around and show her car off. She saw a twenty-two-year-old man she'd met the week before and innocently asked him if he'd like to go for a ride. He said he would and got in.

She drove to various places around the city and eventually stopped at a skyline view spot. The man started making advances. When she resisted, he beat her into submission and raped her. Afterward, her attacker pressed a screwdriver against her neck and forced her into the trunk of her car. He then drove her car along the road looking for an entrance to a nearby regional park.

Police files contain many cases of unsolved murders in which a woman has been raped and killed and her body buried in a remote area. This girl did not panic, feel overwhelmed, or react like a victim, however. She came up with a survival plan. It was very dark out, almost midnight. She found the wires to the taillights and ripped them out.

Two police officers saw the car driving by with no taillights and decided to investigate. When they stopped the car and approached it, they heard the girl pounding inside the trunk and shouting for help. The officers freed the girl and arrested the man.

A police sergeant said, "I think the highlight is the girl's moxie to work her way through the ordeal. She'd already been physically and sexually assaulted. She showed incredible survival instincts to get out of this without panicking."

Tension Affects Efficiency

The relationship between efficiency and tension can be plotted on a graph as shown below:

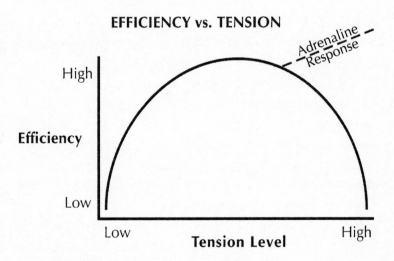

EFFICIENCY vs. TENSION

At low levels of arousal a person is slow to respond. Many people can't get going without their morning coffee. At high levels of arousal a person makes mistakes. She reacts too fast, panics, and loses control.

The exception, indicated by the dotted line in the graph, is for an action requiring a simple, powerful, adrenaline-fueled muscular effort, such as that Alison Wright demonstrated when removing herself from the bus crash with only her upper body strength.

Laughing Improves Efficiency

Playful humor enhances survival for many reasons. Mental efficiency is directly related to a person's general level of emotional arousal. People are less able to solve problems and make precise, coordinated movements when strongly worked up. Laughing reduces tension to more moderate levels and efficiency improves.

Susanne Eneya was driving to an evening meeting when the driver's side of her car was hit broadside by another car. She told me her first thought after the accident was, "Damn! I'm going to miss my meeting."

The rescue workers had grim looks on their faces when they saw how the metal frame of her car was crushed down on her. They had to cut her car apart to get her out. Even though her pelvis and ribs were fractured she kept trying to reassure them, "I'm going to be all right. Don't look so serious. I'm going to be all right." She told them to be careful and not cut her new coat.

The emergency room surgeon looked dispirited when he saw her. In most accidents like hers the person has internal bleeding. He was afraid he would have to operate. Susanne tried to get him and the nurses to relax by joking with them about their names. When they told her they were going to cut her clothing off, she wouldn't let them. Although painful, she made them pull off her sweater, skirt, and panties. When the doctor was about to cut off her bra, she said to him, "Don't cut off my bra. Think back to being in high school. Just reach back and unsnap it!" She says he laughed and finally loosened up. Susanne did not need surgery and eventually recovered fully.*

Playfulness Is Powerful

Playing with a situation makes a person more powerful than sheer determination. The person who toys with the situation creates an inner feeling of "This is my plaything; I am bigger than it. I can toy with it as I wish. I won't let it scare me. I'm going to have fun with this."

The owner of a high-volume cash business says that occasionally a government agent will walk in and demand immediate access to all his records. Having gone through this many times in over thirty years, he sits back and thinks to himself: "I'm paying your salary. Come on, give me your best shot. I want to see how good you are." He listens and jokes with the agent about how much time the agent will spend only to end up with nothing. He does not reveal that he has a law degree and knows exactly what government agents can and cannot do. He also knows that he runs an honest business, so he remains relaxed and enjoys playing with each encounter.

Playfulness Provides Perspective

Playful humor can also give a person a different, less frightening perspective. It can redefine a situation. For example, a woman

---

*For a full account of Susanne's story, see the survivor story archives at www.THRIVEnet.com.

told me that while she and her husband were away on an overnight trip their house had burned to the ground. It was a total loss. The next morning she and some neighbors stood looking at the smoldering ruins. The neighbors were tense and quiet. She said, "That's a hell-of-a-way to get rid of the cockroaches and mice." When they looked at her strangely, she just shrugged.

The person who makes humorous observations is relaxed, alert, and focused outward toward the situation to be dealt with. When former President Ronald Reagan was shot in an assassination attempt, the bullet entered through his left armpit at a vulnerable spot above his bulletproof vest. His bodyguards shoved him into the limousine and slammed the door. As the limousine sped away, heading for the nearest hospital, Reagan said, "Did anyone find out what that guy's beef is?"

The surgeons were scrubbed and ready when Reagan was wheeled into surgery. He looked at them in their masks and gowns and said, "I hope you're all Republicans!"

When his wife, Nancy, visited him in the recovery room, she asked how he was. He answered with a famous quote from a W. C. Fields movie: "All things considered, I'd rather be in Philadelphia."

And finally, another benefit of playful humor is that it leads to the discovery of creative solutions.

Experience Counts, There Is No Formula

The value of laughing depends on the situation at hand. Sometimes laughing is the right thing to do, other times it is not suitable. Sometimes one person will laugh when others do not, often creating an uncomfortable situation. There is no formula for it; it's a matter of experience and judgment.

Some situations may be so upsetting that laughing is not possible. If so, the person with a survivor orientation may curse to reduce tension and bring emotions under control. The purpose, as with laughing, is to free your mind to understand and find practical ways of responding to the crisis. If you find yourself in this situation, allow yourself to get mad, release your tension, and then move on.

A Commitment to Move Forward

When problems or setbacks occur, the better survivors recover quickly from feeling discouraged. They don't waste time dwelling on the past or on what they've lost. Their full energies are directed toward getting things to turn out well in the present and the future. The following statements typify their attitudes:

- There's no going back—go on the best way possible.

- No one can tell me what I can't do.

- Life isn't fair. Big deal. You play the hand of cards you were dealt.

- What would I do if my life was totally disrupted by disaster? Start over again.

Such statements reveal that emotional survival includes overcoming feelings of anger at the world for not treating them fairly. The best survivors spend almost no time, especially in emergencies, getting upset about what has been lost, or feeling distressed about things going badly. They can let go and start over. They know that if they lose everything, they will still have themselves.

They know they will move forward from the experience. For this reason they don't usually take themselves too seriously and are therefore hard to threaten. In fact, they may be amused at threats to their jobs, property, or reputations.

The Power of Commitment and Self-Confidence

The survivor way of orienting to a crisis is to feel fully and totally personally responsible for making things work out well. The better your self-confidence, the more you can face up to a crisis believing that you can handle it without knowing exactly what you will do. When you keep at it, play with it, and allow yourself to do something unpredictable, you usually discover or invent a way to deal effectively with the dangers—and may have energy to help others as well.

Self-confidence lets you feel comfortable in ambiguous situations. You can move into unknown territories—mental, physical, or emotional—and be curious about what you will discover. This ability to operate in the unknown comes from being able to demand a great deal from yourself. You can count on your own stamina, creativity, and ability to hold up in the worst situations.

Learn from the Outcome

Think back to a crisis or emergency you went through. Describe what happened, how you reacted, and what you did. Without criticizing yourself, think about (1) what you could do to avoid a similar crisis again and (2) how you could handle yourself better if something like that were to happen again.

The Survival Style

The everyday habits of life's best survivors include curiosity, playfulness, empathy, needing to have things work well, feeling completely responsible for their lives working well, and learning how to influence events to result in good outcomes. Serendipitously, it is this style of living your life that is also the best style for handling survival situations. Self-talk stabilizes extreme emotions. Questions draw in essential information. Playfulness reduces tension, provides perspective, and can lead to a practical course of action.

Life's best survivors will act logically or, if no reasonable alternative seems available, may do something irrational. It is likely at these times that those close to them have a hard time understanding them.

THIRTEEN

Surviving Being a Survivor

I KNEW I was right," the thin, pale man wearing an old blue sweater declared, grinning at me. His eyes glowed with joy. "The other managers at my company say I'm negative, but I'm not. I'm more determined to be successful than they are. Your workshop today proves that I'm right. I've tried to tell them that for us to succeed with a new product, we should try to anticipate all the problems we might encounter. But they don't listen. They dismiss me as a pessimist and then make big blunders." He shook his head and looked down. "It's strange. I know I'm better at anticipating and avoiding problems than they are, but they're convinced that their gung-ho way of thinking is superior to mine."

Coping with the Challenges of Being a Survivor

It is not unusual for people with survivor personalities to be misunderstood by others. Some feel like misfits. The key issue is whether to act right, trying to stay within the comfort level of others, or to act in ways that work well even when it means ruffling a few feathers.

Life's best survivors know that their way is not standard operating procedure (SOP), but they must be true to themselves despite the drawbacks. Among the many challenges that a true survivor often faces are:

- **Being misunderstood.** Others may misunderstand your paradoxical traits. People who think in either/or ways are not able to appreciate your ability to think in both one way and the opposite. If you voice your opinion of what you see as others' limited visions, you may be labeled as a negative troublemaker who isn't a team player. Do your best to be understood, but accept that not everyone will get you.

- **Having your empathetic nature misinterpreted.** Others seldom comprehend how you can empathize with an unpopular view while not agreeing with it. If you are a person who listens with understanding to an opposing group, you run the risk of becoming an outcast.

  In a face-to-face situation, if you see merit in another person's point of view, he may mistakenly think you are willing to acquiesce to his way. Some people cannot distinguish between empathy and agreement. You may need to be overt: repeat his reasoning back to him, adding, "I understand what you are saying but I don't agree with it."

- **Becoming overly sensitive.** Empathy exposes you to distress and pain in others. Having too much subliminal sensitivity can set you up to pick up other people's fears and distress and you confuse their feelings with your own. Give yourself time to discern the meaning and origin of the feelings you sense. For example, the next time you are stuck in traffic, check to see if the angry feelings are yours or may actually be coming from the many other drivers nearby. You may need to do some insensitivity training with yourself.

- **Learning about yourself can be painful.** When you practice empathy—seeing both sides of an argument or situation— you may uncover truths about yourself that are less than flattering, such as hypocrisy, prejudice, or short-sightedness. At times you may feel stupid and remorseful. It is important, however, not to forget to learn from and make the most of your self-discoveries and insights.

- **Experimenting is uncomfortable.** The more new things and ways of thinking you try, the less confident you may feel about your own maturity. Making mistakes and feeling uncomfortable in any situation is part of the growing up— and it is a life-long process. Embrace it.

- **Taking responsibility for your prejudices.** Developing more survivor qualities may require recognizing and giving up restrictions on your own upsetting opposites. You may now be aware of yourself acting, thinking, or feeling in ways you previously condemned in others. For example, if you used to ridicule others for reporting intuitive experiences, unless you decide to drop your prejudice and open up to the possibility that maybe some of these reports actually had value to them, you will usually find it difficult to accept your own intuitive experiences. You need to stretch your self-concept to accept new things about yourself. You may discover that qualities you criticized in others could have value for you.

- **Being invalidated by others.** It is common for people to play Monday morning quarterback to your survival story, intimating that what action you did or did not take was wrong and that they would have done things differently. Whether it is from ego or fear, it is hard for some people to simply accept that another has demonstrated survival skills that they themselves may lack or think are wrong. Former freelance journalist Jill Carroll was held hostage for eighty-two days in Baghdad. Every aspect of her life was controlled—when to eat, sleep, stand, sit, talk, use the toilet, and so on. After her release she recalled how, to survive her ordeal, she had to give up the strong sense of self she had developed over her life and become completely compliant to her captors. It was either that or be killed. When she returned to the United States, it took her some time to regain her self-confidence and ability to make her own decisions. She was often asked how she could have been so complacent and go along with demands such as being forced to make a propagandistic video. Jill knew she did what she had to do in the circumstance, and it kept her alive. Employing your strong inner selfs will allow you to brush off these sorts of criticisms.

- **Being seen as disloyal for trying to make things better.** Responsible, ethical, loyal employees who go through proper organizational channels to report concerns about organizational misconduct, fraudulent reports, unsafe products, unethical or illegal activities often get themselves into trouble. Instead of being thanked, they are told not to rock the boat. If they don't heed the warning, they are seen as disloyal or not a team player. (The same can be said for the whistle-blower who goes public with organizational wrongdoing and suffers the consequences of being ostracized, fired, or harassed.)

- **Rejecting help or advice, won't talk with others.** A highly self-sufficient, internally focused person can be so determined to go it alone, he may refuse help, which could be very useful. He may believe that because he survived the acute physical challenge of preserving his life by himself, he can handle all the mental challenges that come afterward alone as well. For example, older generations of combat veterans who were not dealing well with their memories of extreme war experiences often refused to talk with counselors or participate in support groups. Many of these soldiers ended up homeless with debilitating mental disorders. Nowadays, the Department of Defense has developed resiliency programs (accessible through www.TRICARE.mil) to help veterans from all branches of the armed services with their mental health issues. Support groups exist for survivors of nearly every kind of traumatic experience. Joining one, even for a short time, can help you talk through your experiences and have a focused session on learning directly from the experiences of others.

- **Having always to be strong.** Others may expect you to be strong all the time. They won't allow you to have moments of weakness or give you the nurturing or support they always expect to get from you. You may have to practice asking for help from those close to you when you need support and letting others know about your needs.

- **Having others ask too much of you.** After Joy Blitch spoke at conferences about how she recovered from cancer, she would be awakened at two and three in the morning by telephone calls from people wanting her help for themselves or someone else who had cancer. Other people may come to think that you have survival energy that can be bestowed upon them, like hands-on healing. These demands can become an unwelcome burden, especially when you care about the welfare of others.

- **Becoming the object of envy.** When you become good at making things work well in your life, some people claim you are just lucky. You have to brace yourself for some jabs and cheap shots from those who believe that because you make it look easy—it is. You have to learn to accept this behavior (demonstrating once again your empathy) and *give yourself credit*.

- **Outclassing yourself.** People who have once owned and run their own businesses, for example, seldom fit in as employees in large corporations. Veterans, who at the age of nineteen were making fast life-and-death decisions and handling thousands of dollars worth of supplies, have a hard time in their twenties tolerating long meetings listening to a wimp of a manager lecture them about the cost of using too many paper clips. The competent, effective professional may be a victim of her own confidence and experience, especially if a boss or superior feels threatened. The best solution to this is to find a person or two you can talk with who can relate to your situation. While you may have to put up with certain circumstances in one area of your life, having others to turn to occasionally as a relief valve is a valuable asset.

- **Getting tough.** To make things work well may require not always being the nice guy. Sometimes you may need to refuse to help people who create their own nonlife-threatening problems. Sometimes the best course of action is to let others struggle and try to resolve their issues on their own. You may just need to hold back and let others suffer the consequences of their actions.

- **Being unable to quit.** By being so determined to master a situation, you may refuse to give up, even when it would be wise to do so. A person with highly evolved survival skills may have to consciously review how worthwhile an effort is. What would happen if you let it go? Learn to know when to fold 'em.

- **Feeling survivor guilt.** At the Vietnam Veteran's Memorial Wall in Washington, DC, I came upon a man clearly in deep distress. I stood with him while he quietly sobbed. After a few minutes he looked at me, touched the wall, and said, "It should be my name there, not theirs. I'd gladly trade my life for them to still be alive." Those who survive layoffs in the workplace often feel this same kind of guilt. They feel guilty about still having a job when friends from work who have more difficult lives are now struggling with unemployment. Survivor guilt can be lessened by challenging irrational thoughts. Often the remaining survivors believe there was something more they could have done to prevent the event or circumstance, when in reality there wasn't. Talking with others about the situation can help you regain perspective.

- **Outgrowing others.** When you develop better and more well-integrated ways of thinking, feeling, and acting, you may outgrow friends and loved ones. This may even mean that a spouse, colleague, or longtime friend is no longer someone with whom you want to maintain emotional contact. You may want to alter a relationship to avoid being stifled, drained, or exploited. The easiest way is to simply decide not to discuss certain issues with the person. If altering the relationship is not possible, you may need to reevaluate it with regard to your future. Make two lists: one of the positive aspects of the relationship and one of the negative. Recognizing and evaluating the strengths and weaknesses of the situation will help you put it into perspective and decide whether or not it is worth continuing.

- **Being criticized for being selfish.** When you attempt to pull out of a relationship that is no longer working, others may try all manner of tricks to make you feel responsible for their well-being and take advantage of your empathy for them.

    Taking steps to change things for the better in your life may throw other people out of their habit patterns and force them to make changes *they* didn't want to make. They may blame you for their distress. It requires a unique form of courage to act when you are empathetic to other people, especially when they blame you for their own predicament. Just keep in mind that their insensitivity to you and their inability to handle difficulties is partly why you are pulling away.

- **Feeling lonely.** Because of your unique, complex nature, you may feel a longing for someone who really understands you. But as you become more capable, the less dependent you may be on others. Highly competent, intelligent women, for example, typically find that the better they get, the harder it is to find a partner equal to them. Finding people you can relate to takes some effort. Joining professional organizations or other highly specialized groups can help you find like-minded folks. In addition, these days, there's a specialized dating service for nearly every interest.

Being Abnormal Is Okay

When I taught introductory psychology, I would give students the following assignment, "Write a short paper explaining why an exceptionally mentally healthy person is abnormal." Most students would frown, look puzzled, and say, "Huh?"

Usually, however, by the time they completed the paper and we discussed the issue in class, most of them came to realize that *normal* does not mean good or right or healthy. It means average. Anyone who deviates far from the norm is, technically speaking, an abnormal person.

Men, for many decades, have made a big mistake in believing that because women appear to be so unpredictable, there must be something wrong with them. My friend the psychiatric nurse who said she appreciated learning about her paradoxes admitted, "It's good to know it's not weird—I used to puzzle myself."

It is ironic how often people with well-developed survivor qualities fear they are mentally unstable when they are, in truth, exceptionally mentally healthy.

The Next Steps

A thousand years from now this period in history will be seen as the time when the human race awakened from the dark ages of its consciousness. Students taking tests will write: "The start of the twenty-first century marked the transformation to integrated consciousness. Until then, human societies were dominated by an inflexible way of thinking."

Transformation means to change from one form to another. When one looks, it is easy to see many signs that the human race is transforming to its next stage of development. People are finding that their survival and well-being depends on breaking free from old ways of thinking and functioning that are no longer useful. In the *old form*, or pattern, human societies have been controlled by a rigid thinking pattern that based each person's identity on an external frame of reference. The *new form* is emerging as humans achieve a higher level of development based on each person's internal frame of reference.

What you may be confronted with in the future as a survivor and what you develop as your unique combination of strengths and capabilities are for you to discover. Only you can do it. Thriving often depends on how well you can comprehend a new reality and do something that works—for you.

FOURTEEN

Your Transformation

Learning About Surviving and Thriving

No book, no workshop, no training program can teach you how to develop your own version of a survivor personality. The more you allow some workshop leader or an author who has never met you to try to shape you into being a more ideal person, the less chance you have of developing your own surviving and thriving skills. Keep in mind also that my book—like all writings about surviving, resiliency, hardiness, thriving, coping, or whatever—describes what I have found worked in the past, for others, in situations that may never exist again.

A Survivor Personality Can't Be Taught but It Can Be Learned

Inspired by books like this one, you can create a self-managed plan for developing qualities and skills that will improve your ability to handle change, unexpected challenges, and disruptive crises that come your way. In your personal plan you may want to consider some of the following:

- **Ask questions.** Respond to change, new developments, threats, confusion, trouble, or criticism by asking, What is happening? Develop a curiosity reflex. In this way you can practice reading each new situation rapidly.

- **Increase your mental and emotional flexibility.** Tell yourself, "It is all right to feel and think in both one way and the opposite." Free yourself from the inner voices of your past that say you shouldn't feel or think a certain way. Develop many response choices for yourself.

- **Assume that change and having to work with uncertainty and ambiguity are a way of life from now on.** Learn to handle change with self-confidence. Experiment with reactions and note consequences. You will find that the lessons you learned in the past about change can be applied—and altered if necessary—to new developments to get them to work out well. In today's world, getting good results counts more than working hard, so build on what you already know.

- **Learn how to learn from all experiences.** Learning is the antidote to feeling victimized. When you learn to see difficult people and events as your teachers in the school of life, you can examine your vulnerabilities and blind spots and learn how to handle yourself better. The more you take from these encounters, the more capable and effective you become.

- **Develop empathy.** Put yourself in the other person's place. Ask, What does she feel and think? What are her views, assumptions, explanations, and values? How does she benefit from acting as she does? Often you will have more success in dealing with others if you govern your actions not blindly by what *you* want to have happen, but by being in tune to how others react to what you do or want, and adjust accordingly. In addition, if you practice sincere thankfulness to those who give you unpleasant feedback, you will develop your understanding of the motivations behind their actions.

- **Resist putting labels on others.** In every encounter you should observe and describe what others say and do to give you insight into what they currently think and feel. If you use negative nouns when you want to swear at someone ("You are a jerk") and positive nouns when you want to praise him ("You are a saint"), recognize that these labels restrict your ability to see changes in his behavior that may affect your situation. Once you've put a label on someone, you unconsciously look for ways to reinforce your perception and could be blinded to or dismissive of subtle changes the person makes. One of these changes could be the key to freeing up the new idea or direction you need to solve a problem or change a behavior. By describing someone by his reaction ("You *acted* like a jerk"), you make it easier to reevaluate that person at a future time when his actions change.

- **Take time to observe and reflect.** Take several deep breaths. Scan your feelings. Be alert to fleeting impressions and the early clues about what might be happening around you.

- **Make yourself useful in all situations.** Ask yourself, "What can I do so that things work well for everyone?" Your ability to find ways to be useful *makes you valuable*—and valued.

- **Take time to appreciate yourself.** Appreciate your accomplishments. Feelings of positive self-regard help blunt the sting of hurtful criticism. Your self-esteem determines how much you learn in difficult situations. The stronger your self-esteem, the more you learn.

- **Follow the surviving and thriving sequence.** Regain emotional balance, adapt and cope with your immediate situation, thrive by learning and making things turn out well, and then find the gift. The better you become at this, the faster you can convert disaster into good fortune.

Adversity can lead to the discovery of strengths you did not know you had. An experience seen as emotionally toxic for others can be made emotionally nutritious for you. A difficulty that almost breaks your spirit can be turned into one of the best things that ever happened to you. It is all up to you—your attitude and your willingness to expand your repertoire of available reactions will determine how well you survive life's most difficult challenges.

CITATIONS

1. Life Is Not Fair

Julius Segal quotation is from his book *Winning Life's Toughest Battles* (Ivy Books, 1986).

Charlie Plumb quotation is from a transcript of an interview on NBC, June 24, 1986.

Nietszche quotation is from Victor Frankl's *Man's Search for Meaning* (Beacon, 2006).

2. Playful Curiosity

Maria Montessori quotation is from her book *The Absorbent Mind* (Holt, Rinehart & Winston, 1967).

Robert W. White's article is "Motivation Reconsidered: The Concept of Competence," *The Psychological Review* 66 (1959).

Robert Fulghum quotation is from his book *All I Really Need to Know I Learned in Kindergarten* (Ivy Books, 1986).

Daniel Goleman quotation is from his book *Emotional Intelligence* (Bantam, 2005).

Carole Hyatt and Linda Gottlieb quotation is from their book *When Smart People Fail* (Simon and Schuster, 2009).

3. Flexibility

T. C. Schneirla's explanation of biphasic pattern of adjustment is from his article "An Evolutionary and Developmental Theory of Biphasic Process Underlying Approach and Withdrawal," reprinted in *Selected Writings of T. C. Schneirla* (Freeman, 1972; originally published 1959).

Lorus J. Milne and Margery Milne quotation is from their book *Patterns of Survival* (Prentice-Hall, 1967).

Aron Ralston story is from personal communications, his book *Between a Rock and a Hard Place* (Atria, 2004), and "How He Survived," *Oregonian*, May 9, 2003.

Moshe Feldenkrais quotation is from his book *Awareness Through Movement* (Harper & Row, 1972).

4. The Synergy Imperative

Mihaly Csikszentmihaly's discussion of flow is from his book *Flow: The Psychology of the Optimal Experience* (Harper Perennial, 2008).

Ruth Benedict's discussion of synergy is from "Synergy: Some Notes of Ruth Benedict," *American Anthropologist* 72 (1970).

José Ortega y Gasset's ideas are from *The Revolt of the Masses* (Norton, 1957; originally published c. 1932).

Abraham Maslow quotation is from his book *The Farther Reaches of Human Nature* (Viking, 1971).

Anthony Robbins quotation is from his newsletter "Sharing Ideas" (December 1992/January 1993).

5. Empathy

Arnold Toynbee quotation is from his book *Surviving the Future* (Oxford Press, 1971).

Joe Dibello's story is from the *Oregonian*, January 7, 1996.

6. The Survivor's Edge

Weston H. Agor quotation is from his article "How Top Executives Use Their Intuition to Make Important Decisions," *Business Horizons* (January/ February 1986).

Roy Rowan quotation is from his book *The Intuitive Manager* (Little, Brown, 1986).

Winston Churchill's story is from Violet Bonham Carter's *Winston Churchill: An Intimate Portrait* (Harcourt, Brace, 1965).

Robert Godfrey quotation is from his book *Outward Bound: Schools of the Possible* (Anchor Books, 1980).

Harold Sherman quotation is from his book *How to Make ESP Work for You* (Fawcett-Crest, 1964).

Carol Burnett's story is from an interview on *The Charles Grodin Show* (CNBC, May 1995).

Gillian Holloway's method is from *Dreaming Insights: A 5-Step Plan for Discovering the Meaning in Your Dream* (Practical Psychology Press, 2002).

Lieutenant Iceal Hambleton's account is from William Anderson's *Bat-21* (Bantam Books, 1980).

Sarnoff Mednick was developing his Remote Associations Test while I was in graduate school at the University of Michigan. His copyrighted version has high validity.

Emile Coué was quoted in John Duckworth's *How to Use Auto-Suggestion Effectively* (Wilshire, 1972).

Alex F. Osborn quotation is from his book *Your Creative Power* (Dell, 1948).

Howard Stephenson quotation is from his book *They Sold Themselves* (Hillman-Curl, 1937).

Christopher Glenn's article is "Natural Disasters and Human Behavior: Explanation, Research and Models," *Psychology: A Quarterly Journal of Human Behavior* 16, no. 2 (1979).

7. The Serendipity Talent

Horace Walpole's coining of the word *serendipity* is described in Theodore Remer's *Serendipity and the Three Princes: From the Peregriniaggio of 1557* (University of Oklahoma, 1965).

Lance Armstrong's story is from media accounts and his books written with Sally Jenkins, *It's Not About the Bike* (Putnam/Berkley, 2001) and *Every Second Counts* (Broadway, 2004).

8. The Good-Child Handicap

Good noun discussion is from personal communications with Larry Mathae and his unpublished manuscript "The Good Guy, Bad Guy Code of the West." See also the passages on being nice in George Bach and Herb Goldberg's *Creative Aggression* (Avon Books, 1974).

Anne Wilson Schaef's pioneering activities and her books *Women's Reality: An Emerging Female System* (HarperOne, 1992) and *Co-Dependence: Misunderstood, Mistreated* (HarperOne, 1992) gave rise to the co-dependency movement. There are now dozens of books on the subject.

Shale Paul's views on codependency are from his book *The Warrior Within: A Guide to Inner Power* (Delta Group Press, 1983).

9. Thriving

Abraham Maslow quotation is from his book *Eupsychian Management* (Irwin & Dorsey, 1965). Republished as *Maslow on Management* (Wiley, 1998).

Employment data is from an unpublished research report by James Pennebaker and associates. Emotions journal information is from James Pennebaker's *Opening Up* (Avon, 1990).

Henry W. Taft quotation is from the preface of Robert Godfrey's *Outward Bound: Schools of the Possible* (Anchor Books, 1980).

Julian Rotter's locus of control discussion and test is from "External Control and Internal Control," *Psychology Today* (June 1971).

Hans Selye quotation is from his book *The Stress of My Life: A Scientist's Memoirs* (Van Nostrand Reinhold, 1979).

11. Self-Managed Healing

Chapter is largely derived from Bernie Siegel's *Love, Medicine, and Miracles* (Harper & Row, 1986).

Caryle Hirshberg and Marc Barasch's spontaneous remission research is from their book *Remarkable Recovery* (Berkeley/Riverhead, 1993).

W. C. Ellerbroek quotation is from "Language, Thought, and Disease," *The Co-Evolution Quarterly* (Spring 1978).

Barbara Marie Brewster quotation is from her book *Journey to Wholeness* (Four Winds, 1992).

Larry King quotation is from "How a Heart Attack Changed Me," *Parade*, January 15, 1989.

Ian Gawler's account is from his books *Peace of Mind* (Avery, 1989) and *You Can Conquer Cancer* (Anderson, 2007), and newspaper articles

obtained from the Yarra Valley Living Centre, Australia. See also www
.Gawler.org.

Howard S. Friedman's information on emotional immunity is from his
book *The Self-Healing Personality* (Henry Holt, 1991). See also Salvatore Maddi and Suzanne Kobasa's book *The Hardy Executive* (Dorsey
Press, 1984).

Hans J. Eysenck's research is from "Health's Character," *Psychology Today*
(December 1988).

Ed Roberts was interviewed in the article "How It's S'pozed to Be" in *This
Brain Has a MOUTH* (July/August 1992; available at www.MouthMag
.com).

Norman Cousins quotation is from his book *Anatomy of an Illness* (W. W.
Norton, 1979).

Bonnie Strickland's presidential address to the American Psychological Association was published as "Internal-External Control Expectancies: From
Contingency to Creativity," *American Psychologist* (January 1989).

Joy Blitch's story is from "What Is Christian Science Treatment?" *Christian
Science Monitor*, August 3, 1990.

O. Carl Simonton, Stephanie Matthews-Simonton, and James L. Creighton's
imaging statistics are from their book *Getting Well Again* (Bantam
Books, 1980).

John D. Evans quotation is from "Imagination Therapy," *The Humanist* 41,
no. 6 (1980).

Louise L. Hay quotation, questions, and results with her PLWA group is
from public lectures and her book *You Can Heal Your Life* (Hay House,
1984).

W. C. Ellerbroek quotation is from "Hypotheses Toward a Unified Field
Theory of Human Behavior with Clinical Application to Acne Vulgaris,"
Perspectives in Biology and Medicine 16, no. 2 (1973).

Emile Coué's work is described in John Duckworth's *How to Use Auto-
Suggestion Effectively* (Wilshire, 1965).

Paul Pearsall's attitude is reflected in his book *Making Miracles: A Scientist's Journey to Death and Back* (Prentice Hall Press, 1991), and other works.

Norman Cousins' concept of fostering healing is from his book *Head First: The Biology of Hope* (E.P. Dutton, 1989).

Mind–body research is from *Mind/Body Medicine: How to Use Your Mind for Better Health* (Consumer Reports, 1993).

Dee Brigham's book on positive visualization is *Imagery for Getting Well* (W. W. Norton, 1994).

Dorothy Woods Smith's comments are from personal communications, www.HousesOfHealing.com, and "Polio and Post-Polio Sequelae: The Lived Experience," *Orthopoedic Nursing* (September/October 1989).

John Callahan quotation is from his book *Don't Worry, He Won't Get Far on Foot* (William Morrow, 1989).

12. Surviving Emergencies and Crises

Alison Wright's story and quotation is from personal communication and her book *Learning to Breathe: One Woman's Journey of Spirit and Survival* (Plume, 2009).

Ben Sherwood's survivor styles are from his book *The Survivor's Club: The Secrets and Science That Could Save Your Life* (Grand Central, 2009).

John Paul Getty quotation is from his book *How to Be Rich* (Playboy, 1966).

Oakland, California, abduction account is from the *San Jose Mercury News*, March 19, 1995.

13. Surviving Being a Survivor

Jill Carroll's hostage account is from the series "The Jill Carroll Story," *Christian Science Monitor*, August 14–28, 2006.

RECOMMENDED READING

Anderson, William. *Bat-21: The Story of Lt. Col. Hambleton.* Bantam Doubleday Dell, 1983.

Anthony, E. James, and Bertram Cohler, eds. *The Invulnerable Child.* Guilford Press, 1987.

Armstrong, Lance, with Sally Jenkins. *Every Second Counts.* Broadway, 2004.

Armstrong, Lance, with Sally Jenkins. *It's Not About the Bike.* Putnam/Berkley, 2001.

Brewster, Barbara Marie. *Journey to Wholeness.* Four Winds, 1992.

Chellis, Marcia. *Ordinary Women, Extraordinary Lives.* Viking Adult, 1992.

Coffee, Gerald. *Beyond Survival.* CEI, 1990.

Csikszentmihalyi, Mihaly. *Flow: The Psychology of the Optimal Experience.* Harper Perennial, 2008.

Des Pres, Terrance. *The Survivors: An Anatomy of Life in the Death Camps.* Oxford University Press, 1976.

Flach, Frederic. *Resilience: Discovering a New Strength at Times of Stress.* Hatherleigh Press, 2004.

Fox, Michael J. *Always Looking Up: The Adventures of an Incurable Optimist.* Hyperion, 2009.

Frankl, Victor. *Man's Search for Meaning.* Beacon, 2006.

Friedman, Howard S. *The Self-Healing Personality.* Henry Holt, 1991.

Goleman, Daniel. *Emotional Intelligence*, Bantam, 2005.

Gonzales, Laurence. *Deep Survival: Who Lives, Who Dies, and Why.* Norton, 2004.

Greenbank, Anthony. *The Book of Survival.* Hatherleigh Press, 2003.

Hamilton, Scott. *The Great Eight: How to Be Happy.* Thomas Nelson, 2009.

Hay, Louise. *You Can Heal Your Life.* Hay House, 1999.

Hyatt, Carole, and Linda Gottleib. *When Smart People Fail.* Simon & Schuster, 2009.

Janifer, Laurence. *Survivor.* Ace, 1977.

Kamler, Kenneth. *Surviving the Extremes.* THUS, 2004.

King, Larry. *My Remarkable Journey.* Weinstein, 2009.

Leslie, Edward E. *Desperate Journeys, Abandoned Souls.* Mariner, 1998.

Lifton, Robert Jay. *The Protean Self.* University of Chicago Press, 1999.

Maddi, Salvatore, and Suzanne Kobasa. *The Hardy Executive.* Irwin Professional, 1984.

Maslow, Abraham. *Maslow on Management.* Wiley, 1998.

Noyce, Wilfrid. *They Survived: A Study of the Will to Live,* Dutton, 1963.

O'Grady, Scott, with Jeff Coplon. *Return With Honor.* Doubleday, 1995.

Paul, Shale. *The Warrior Within: A Guide to Inner Power.* Delta Group, 1983.

Pearsall, Paul. *Making Miracles: A Scientist's Journey to Death and Back.* Prentice Hall, 1991.

Pflug, Jackie Nink, with Peter J. Kizilos. *Miles to Go Before I Sleep.* Hazelden, 2002.

Pink, Daniel H. *A Whole New Mind.* Riverhead, 2006.

Plumb, Charlie. *I'm No Hero.* Executive, 1995.

Ralston, Aron. *Between a Rock and a Hard Place.* Atria, 2005.

Reeve, Christopher. *Still Me.* Ballantine, 1999.

Rowan, Roy. *The Intuitive Manager.* Little, Brown, 1986.

Saldana, Theresa. *Beyond Survival.* Bantam, 1987.

Salk, Jonas. *Survival of the Wisest*. Harper & Row, 1973.

Schemmel, Jerry, with Kevin Simpson. *Chosen to Live*. Victory, 1996.

Segal, Julius. *Winning Life's Toughest Battles: Roots of Human Resilience*. Ivy, 1986.

Seligman, Martin. *Learned Optimism: How to Change Your Mind and Your Life*. Vintage, 2006.

Sherwood, Ben. *The Survivor's Club*. Grand Central, 2009.

Siegel, Bernie. *Faith, Hope and Healing*. Wiley, 2009.

Siegel, Bernie. *Love, Medicine, and Miracles*. Harper & Row, 1986.

Sinetar, Marsha. *Developing a 21st-Century Mind*. Random House, 1991.

Tedeschi, Richard, et al., eds. *Posttraumatic Growth: Positive Changes in the Aftermath of Crisis*. Erlbaum, 1998.

Toynbee, Arnold. *Surviving the Future*. Oxford, 1971.

Troebst, Cord Christian. *The Art of Survival*. Doubleday, 1965.

Walsh, Roger. *Staying Alive*. Shambhala, 1984.

Schaef, Anne Wilson. *Co-Dependence: Misunderstood, Mistreated*. HarperOne, 1992.

Wright, Alison. *Learning to Breathe*. Plume, 2009.

Zar, Rose. *In the Mouth of the Wolf*. Jewish Publication Society, 1983.

ADDITIONAL RESOURCES

All items available through www.PracticalPsychologyPress.com.

Siebert, Al. *The Resiliency Advantage: Master Change, Thrive Under Pressure and Bounce Back from Setbacks* (© Berrett-Koehler, ISBN: 9781576753293).

Siebert, Al. *The Survivor Personality Manual: Guidelines for Facilitating Self-Managed Learning* (© Practical Psychology Press, ISBN: 9780944227008). Coil-bound workbook to accompany *The Survivor Personality*.

Siebert, Al, and Mary Karr. *The Adult Student's Guide to Survival & Success*, 6th ed. (© Practical Psychology Press, ISBN: 9780944227381).

How to Thrive and Grow During Your Job Search [CD-ROM] (© Practical Psychology Press).

Resiliency: The Key to Surviving and Thriving in Today's World [DVD] (© Practical Psychology Press).

Resiliency: The Power to Bounce Back [CD-ROM set] (© Learning Strategies). Personal learning course with workbook.

The Survivor Personality: Why Some People Have a Better Chance of Surviving Than Others [CD-ROM] (© Practical Psychology Press).

For more information, stories, and resources on surviving and thriving, please visit the following websites:

- www.THRIVEnet.com (accompanies *The Survivor Personality*)

- www.SurvivorGuidelines.org (dedicated to the survivors of 9/11 and other terrorist attacks)

- www.ResiliencyCenter.com (accompanies *The Resiliency Advantage*)

- www.AdultStudent.com (accompanies *The Adult Student's Guide to Survival & Success*)

ACKNOWLEDGMENTS

While hundreds of people made this book possible, I wish to give special thanks to the following:

Sam Kimball for countless hours of volunteer editing, encouragement, insightful suggestions, and special friendship.

My mother, who left my mind alone.

My wife, Molly, whose constant love, support, delightful thinking, and belief in me and my work is a deep source of strength for me.

My sister, Mary Karr, and her husband, Chad, for their unflagging support, valuable feedback, and professional expertise.

My youngest niece, Kristin Pintarich, for her outstanding research, writing, and computer skills; intelligent thinking; and excellence in handling details.

Stephanie Abarbanel for her suggestions and encouragement.

Don James, an inspirational writing instructor.

Ruth Aley for her warm encouragement.

Bill Garleb for his friendship and many discussions about surviving.

Enos and Charlott Herkshan for their friendship and teachings.

Bill McKeachie, my teaching mentor.

Jim McConnell, my adviser, writing mentor, and friend.

Hirofumi Hayashida for providing friendship, wisdom, and an international perspective.

Glen Fahs for his desire to see that my work continues to benefit others.

Gillian Holloway for her support, suggestions, and editing.

John Duff for being so perceptive.

All the survivors willing to answer my questions and tell me about their experiences.

Public employees who keep things running while receiving more criticism and less praise than they deserve.

INDEX

Page numbers in **bold** indicate tables; those in *italic* indicate figures or photographs; and those followed by "n" indicate notes.

ABOUT THE AUTHOR

Al Siebert, PhD (1934–2009), founding director of the Resiliency Center, was internationally recognized as an expert on the inner nature of highly resilient survivors. He was an ex-paratrooper with a PhD in psychology from the University of Michigan. He taught management psychology seminars at Portland State University for over thirty years, was a volunteer recovery group leader with Vietnam War veterans, and served as chairman of his county's school board. Articles by him or quotes from his work were often in local and national publications. Siebert was interviewed frequently, including appearances on *The Oprah Winfrey Show*, National Public Radio, CNN, *The Today Show*, and more.

Right up until the end of his life, Siebert showed incredible resiliency and stamina. He was actively involved in training federal managers on resiliency at the Eastern Management Development Center, developing the U.S. Army's Provider Resiliency Training program, serving as a consultant to the World Trade Center Survivor's Network, facilitating local tribal gatherings, and more.

Siebert died of advanced colon cancer. His family would like to encourage everyone to have a colonoscopy near age fifty. When caught early, this condition is often easily survivable, treatable, and preventable.

For more information on Al Siebert and the Resiliency Center, visit www.ResiliencyCenter.com.

For more information about *The Survivor Personality*, visit www .THRIVEnet.com.

CONTRIBUTING EDITORS

Kristin Pintarich has a BA in Communications from Oregon State University and worked alongside Al Siebert for nearly twenty years as his assistant in everything from processing book orders to creating his websites to editing and marketing his works.

Molly Siebert, RHIT, CCS, has an associate degree in science and is pursuing her bachelor's degree in Health Information Technology Management. After six years as marketing director, she now serves as president of the Resiliency Center and assists with the Resiliency Facilitator certification program.